Edited by Catherine McDermott

PLANS AND ELEVATIONS

BEN KELLY DESIGN

Introduction

Catherine McDermott

This book is a celebration of nearly 20 years of work from Ben Kelly. In it we have tried to move away from the usual designer monograph format towards a more open-ended collaboration. During the summer of 1989 friends, colleagues and the team that forms Ben Kelly Design were invited to make a contribution to the text. It seemed appropriate that a designer whose work is so closely bound up in personal relationships should open up the project in this way, allowing the contributors to have control over their own input. These fragments form the text of the book. They reflect creative and diverse personalities touching on theoretical ideas on design to revealing personal reflections. *Plans an Elevations* is divided into four sections each with an abstract title but with a clearly defined structure: education and early work, shop design, media projects, and finally the work for Factory Communications. Ben Kelly Design is a small practice which has built up a close and intimate client list. It is possible they have more professional touchpoints with the Modernists of the 1930s than with the current stockmarket-led approach to contemporary design. They do not compete with the huge design companies. These developments have in some ways pushed Ben Kelly Design to the margins, but their work is not peripheral or exclusive. There is a fair share of private houses but there are also the shops and bars that interact with everyday life. Ben Kelly, Sandra Douglas, Peter Mance and Elena Massucco have painstakingly researched, crafted, and designed the ingredients of a body of work that has helped to define British interior design in the eighties. It is a significant and sometimes underrated achievement. The members of the team fight shy of any kind of analysis, deeply suspicious of a manifesto or label. Instead they invite you to look for yourself at their work.

Guest List

Sir Hugh Casson	Professor, School of Interior Design, Royal College of Art 1952–75 President, Royal Academy 1976–84 Architect
Margaret Casson	Architect, interior and exhibition designer, photographer
Kevin Godley	Musician, songwriter, film and video director, Medialab Production Company
Geoff Hollington	Furniture and product designer Geoff Hollington Associates
Paul Howie	Managing Director, Lynne Franks P.R.
Tony McGee	Fashion photographer and advertising director, Tony McGee Ltd
Paul Mason	General Manager Fac51, The Haçienda Director Fac201, Dry
John Miller	Professor, School of Environmental Design, Royal College of Art 1975–85 Architect, Colquhoun, Miller & Partners
Peter Saville	Co-founder Factory Records. Graphic designer, Peter Saville Associates
Fred Scott	Pre-war, above-average height, writer, teacher and designer. Senior Lecturer, 3-D Design, Kingston Polytechnic
Keith Wainwright	Co-founder Smile hairdressing salon Hairdresser
Ted Walters	Carpenter. Maker/builder of numerous Ben Kelly Design projects Co-founder Morley Walters, Shopfitters – specialist joinery company
Jon Wealleans	Architect, designer Creative Director, Crighton Ltd
Tony Wilson	Co-founder Factory Records Chairman Factory Communications Ltd Director Fac51, The Haçienda Director Fac201, Dry Television presenter and journalist Executive Producer Ancient guru of the avant-garde

1 FROM APPLETREEWICK TO THE WORLDS END

2 INTERNATIONAL ORANGE

3 ALL ALONG THE DOTTED LINE

4 THE HAÇIENDA MUST BE BUILT

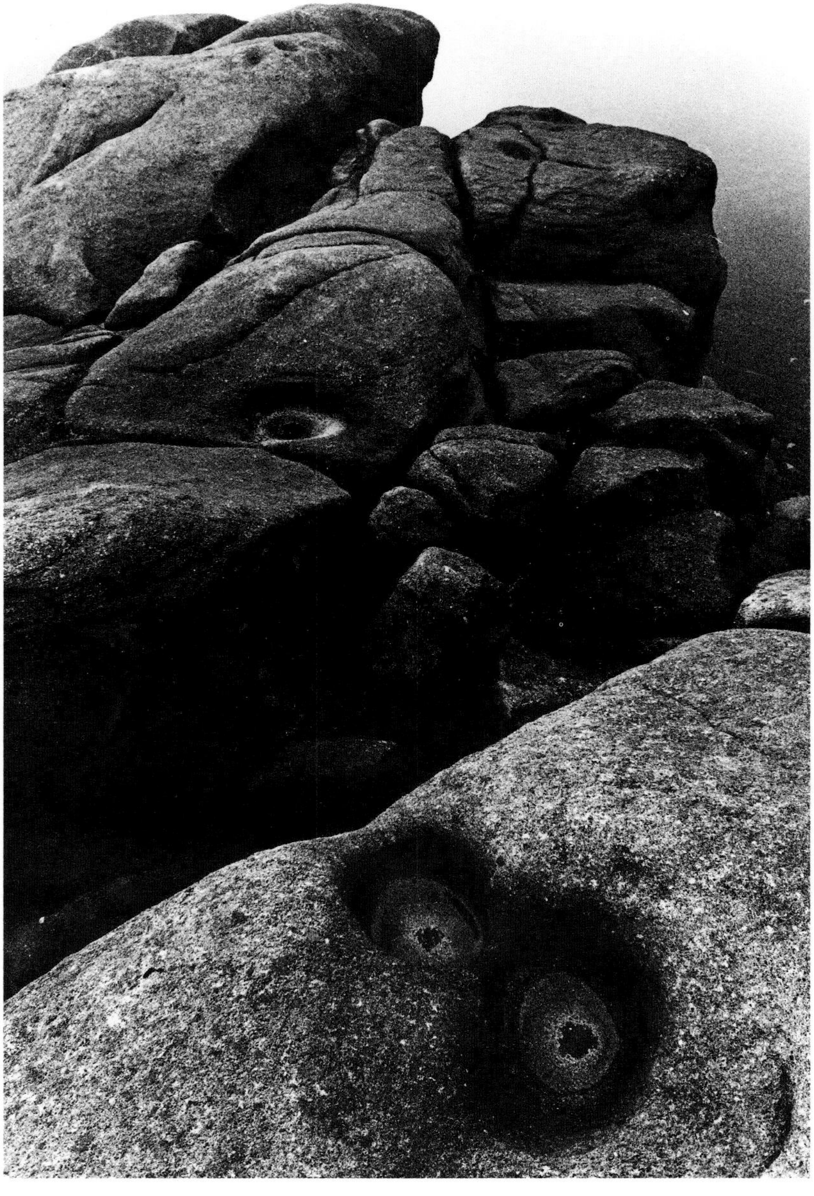

1 FROM APPLETREEWICK TO THE WORLDS END

Ben Kelly

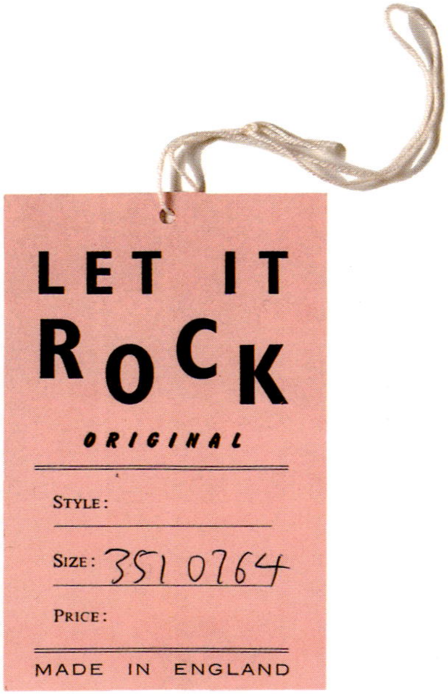

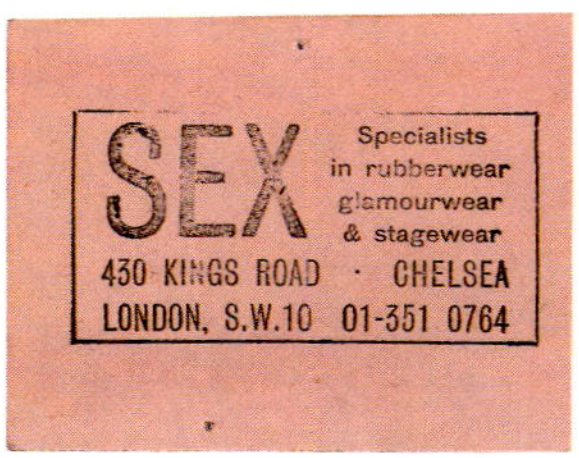

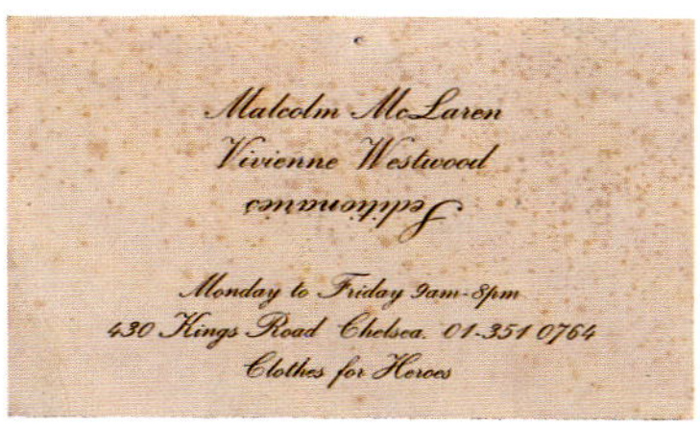

Having arrived at the Worlds End, I needed something to wear. I found it in a shop called Let It Rock. 1971: brothel creepers, fluorescent socks, skin-tight jeans and Mr Freedom.

It was Malcolm and Vivienne's shop. Their attitude was appealing. Malcolm's energy, commitment and madness felt encouraging to someone who had travelled to the metropolis looking for the larger-than-life. From Let It Rock to Sex to Seditionaries. Along the way, over Battenburg cake at a Douggie Fields party, Malcolm suggested he needed a hovel in Dean Street converting into a rehearsal studio and crash pad for some vile group called the Sex Pistols. As soon as the decor had been completed the boys took over and carried out a superb graffiti and demolition job.

Next came the Glitterbest offices, Shaftesbury Avenue; a paint job with a few shelves and filing cabinets. Seditionaries was Malcolm and Vivienne's time bomb. It exploded onto the King's Road like *A Clockwork Orange* betting shop. Malcolm and Vivienne had too many ideas to let anyone else near it. I approached David Connor to do the visuals and interpret Malcolm's idea of bombed-out Dresden. Then David and myself sat down and

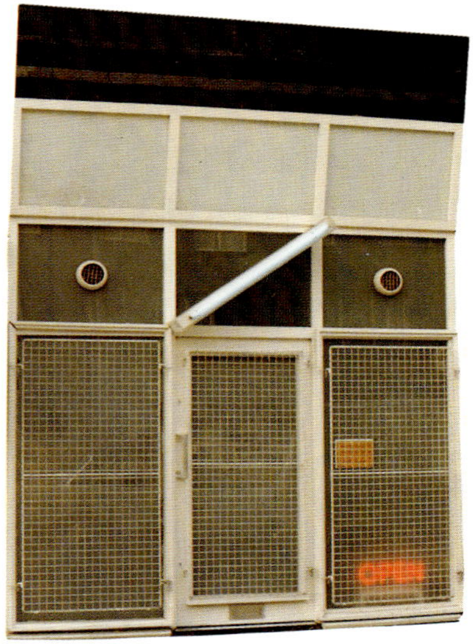

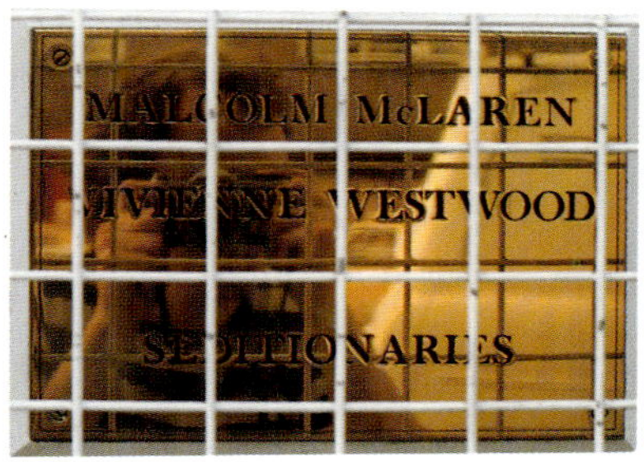

produced the required shopfront. White-flashed opal glass with symmetrical inset circular vents and an angled blue fluorescent above the door. The final touch was a polished brass plaque announcing *Vivienne Westwood Malcolm McLaren Seditionaries*. The safety pins came next.

The legendary guitarist and sex fiend Steve Jones called announcing he had purchased a flat in West Hampstead and needed some work doing. At the 'client meeting' I was confronted by Steve and Paul completely stoned on glue they were using to stick some horrific cork tiles onto the kitchen walls. I came away from the meeting with the following client brief: 'I don't give a shit what you do, as long as it impresses the birds'. One morning most of Hot Gossip trooped out of the bedroom.

The final episode came in the form of an invite to celebrate the release of the Pistols' latest single, *God Save the Queen*, to be premiered at a live gig on a riverboat on Jubilee Day. The occasion came to an abrupt end when the river police forced our boat with its merry revellers back to Charing Cross Pier. The next twelve hours were spent in a cell at Bow Street resulting in a two-year suspended sentence.

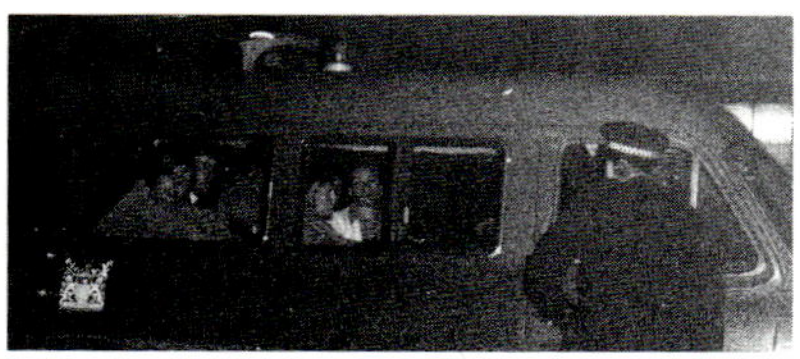

Exit to Bow Street...

Geoff Hollington

Ben is an iconoclast. It seems to me that in his work he has never followed fashion – he's very much on his own trajectory, which refers very little to what is going on around, except when he's debunking conventional wisdom – undermining the accepted way of doing things. If his work has a frame of reference it is the visual arts – fine art – not the world of design.

That's what brought us together in our first week at the Casson's Interior Design School at the Royal College of Art – we wanted to be ARTISTS. Our first collaboration was to collect up all the tasteful gingham drawing board covers, with which Lady Casson had attempted to upgrade the drab first year studio, and stick them to the walls and ceilings in what we imagined was a 'conceptual installation piece'.

Ben and I weren't too keen to spend our three years with the Cassons on *nothing but paper* (plan and elevation) projects – this is a depressing aspect when students in the other RCA schools were building *real things* all around you – so we went our own way, with our 'Art' projects: the Art Bar, Chair Art, two fashion shows, the Lafrance lithographs and an installation in one of the RCA galleries. Which is not to say that we didn't pick up an enthusiasm for architecture, thanks mainly to our tutor John Miller (later to become Professor).

My rebellion confined its attention to the coursework and accepted design values, but Ben's continued over into his social and private lives. His demeanour was often fairly extreme – testing limits: of his metabolism with alcohol and of his definitions of taste with his clothes. I remember him kitted out in late Mr Freedom after a few days in London, but then adopting a modified Teddy Boy style with bits from Malcolm McLaren's first shop.

To graduate from the RCA you had to complete a 'discourse' – a written thesis of some kind. In the liberal early seventies this could be literally anything written, so we both opted for 'creative writing' pieces. Mine was a completely obscure sub-William Burroughs cut-up thing but Ben decided on an autobiographical narrative. In order to make his piece as interesting as Hunter S. Thompson, Ben set out putting himself in the kinds of situations that exemplify Thompson's 'when the going gets weird the weird get going' theory. The paradoxical thing about Ben is that underneath the sometimes manic risk-taker is a very modest, sensible, wary Yorkshire bloke.

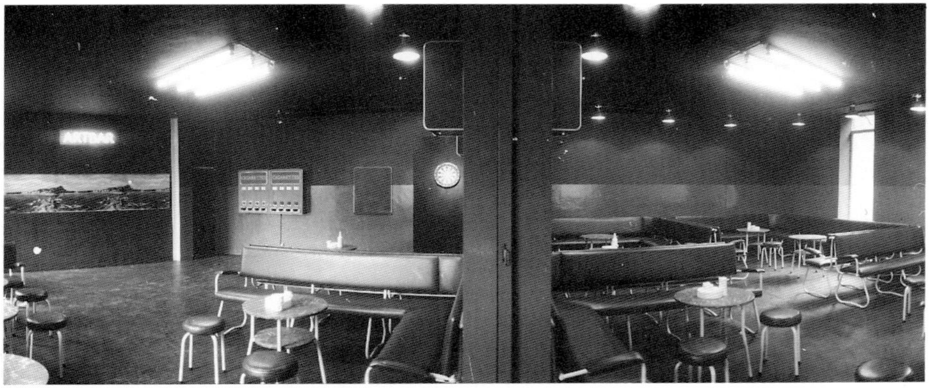

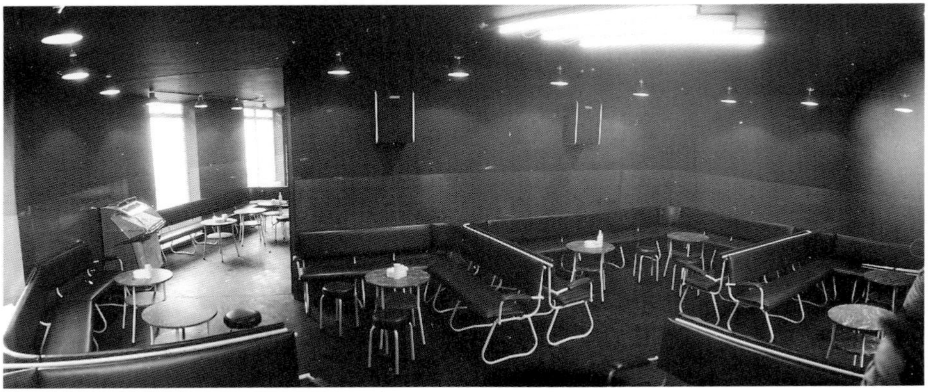

Artbar
RCA students' bar, 1973. The Artbar was revamped on a shoestring. Painted in two shades of bottle green, with a gloss finish up to the dado level. 200 people could sit on tubular frame seating by Baxmander Tubular Productions. The radiators were painted a delicate shade of Milk of Magnesia pink; the barman's uniform in green, buff and pink was designed by Chrissie Walsh, a student in the fashion school. The scheme incorporated a pink neon sign over the bar; black steel conduit; photographic lamps; parallel pink fluorescent strips centred on the diagonal. Ceramic ashtrays incorporating beer bottles, beer cans, a pint mug, a cigarette packet and lighter were designed by Robin Levien. Joint project, Geoff Hollington and Ben Kelly.

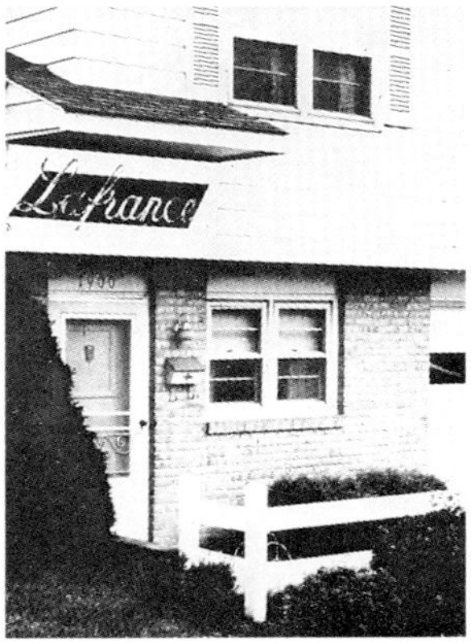

Lafrance
Executed as a set of eight four-colour photolitho prints, 1972/73. Lafrance is a house, or rather the suggestion of a house in which all aspects of interior domestic architecture have been substituted by their public building counterparts. A stairway becomes an escalator; the dining room is furnished like a café; sanitary accomodation includes urinal stalls; and crockery is stamped with a house logo such as might be found in an hotel or a restaurant. Joint project, Geoff Hollington and Ben Kelly.

A Ware, B Ware, Y Ware
In the spring of 1975 Robin Levien approached two friends, Ben Kelly and Geoff Hollington. ex-students of the Environmental Design School. He proposed the idea of forming a team to evolve a system or formula which could be used to solve any visual design problem – a method with which Ben and Geoff had already experimented. The work shown here is the result of the system's application to ceramics.

A
WARE
LONDON

A Ware is a range of domestic items chosen for their quasi-decorative function, allowing scope for the application of a primarily visual design system. The pieces are intended for volume production and this has fixed their visual character.

B
WARE
LONDON

B Ware is an extension of A Ware into a limited range of studio pieces. The system is modified to give a broader framework allowing the use of colour, applied decoration and additional materials. In each piece the secondary material (i.e. glass, metal, marble, wood) supports the ceramic component and expresses an exaggerated dynamic.

Y
WARE
LONDON

Y Ware is an artwork, undertaken in the same frame of minds.

B Ware Vase
207mm x 190mm x 160mm.
The main body is mauve glazed ceramic, supported by an angled glass slab with polished edges. The glass is bolted to the vase using a nylon nut, bolt and washer, and acts as a secondary support material. The main ceramic body tapers to a conical base and sits on a rubber foot. The vase is 'decorated' with a gold B Ware transfer and the word VASE is set in relief.

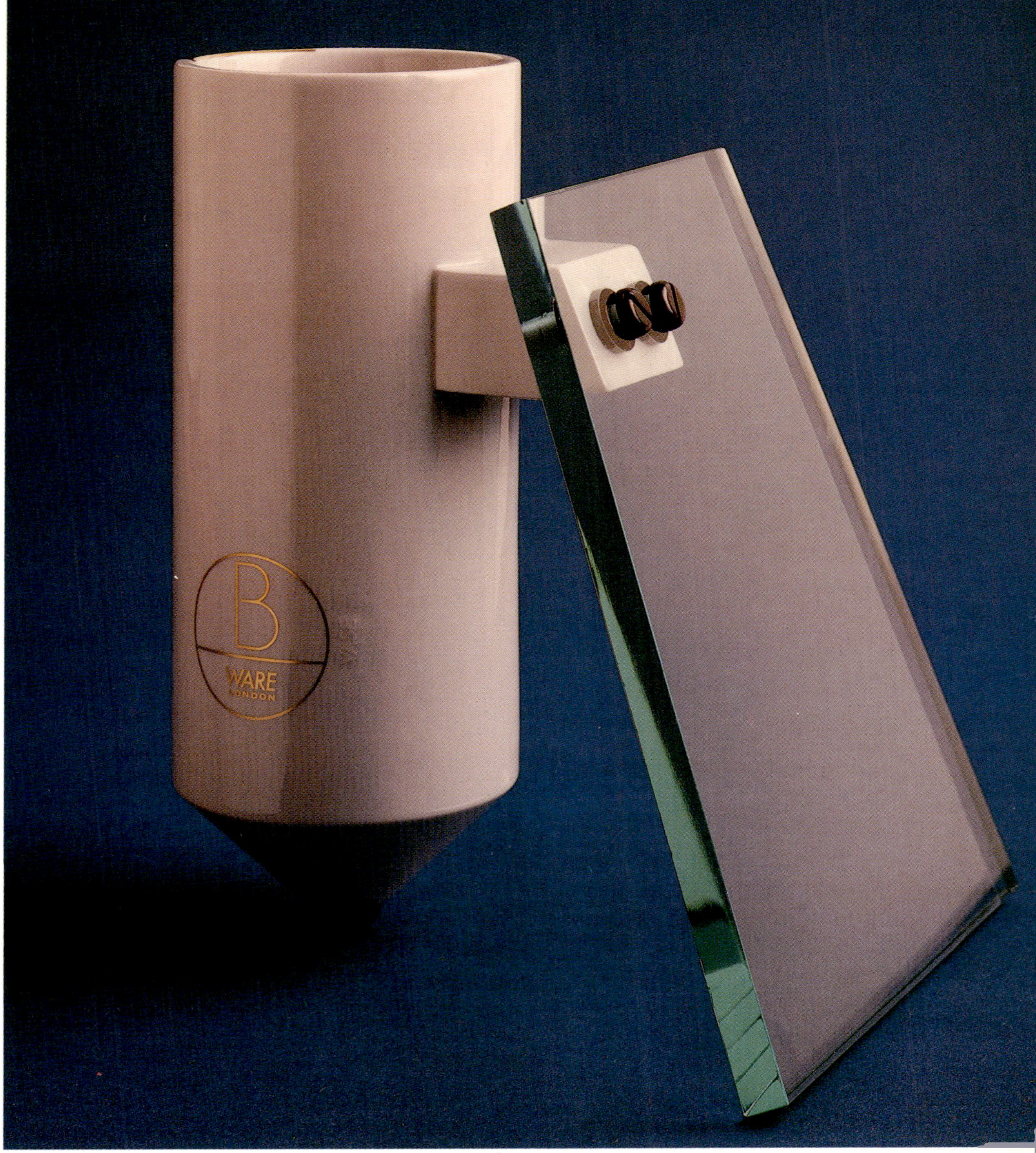

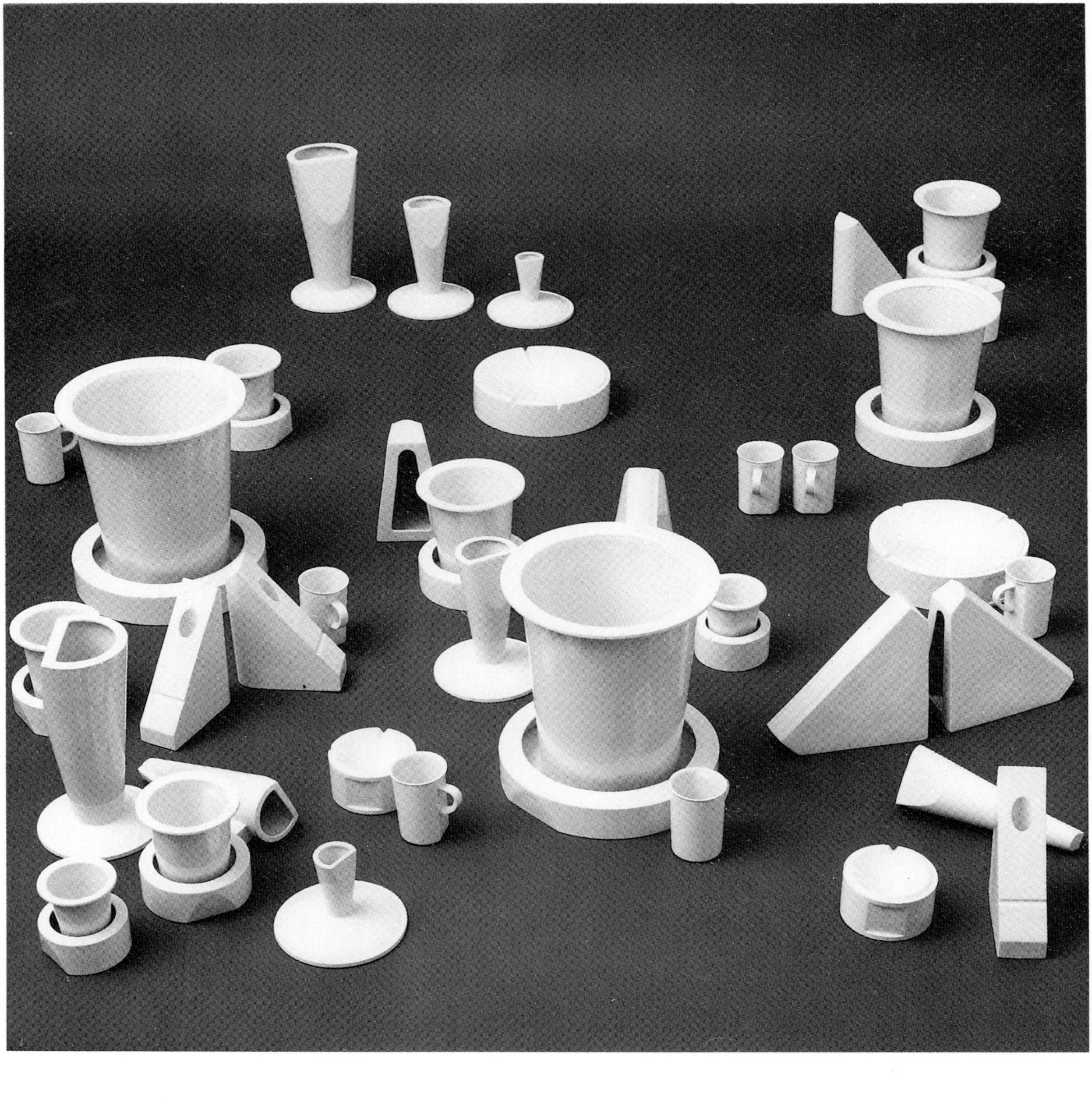

A Ware LEFT
A range of white slipcast ceramics – what the market chooses to call 'giftware'. The 'committee' designed the A Ware elements in the course of a year, having first established a brief or manifesto. A Ware was conceived based on explicit principles and not conceptualised after the event. 'All pieces feature a sliced-off flat' stamped with the A Ware logo. The seams where the moulds break are allowed to remain and feature as integral to each piece.

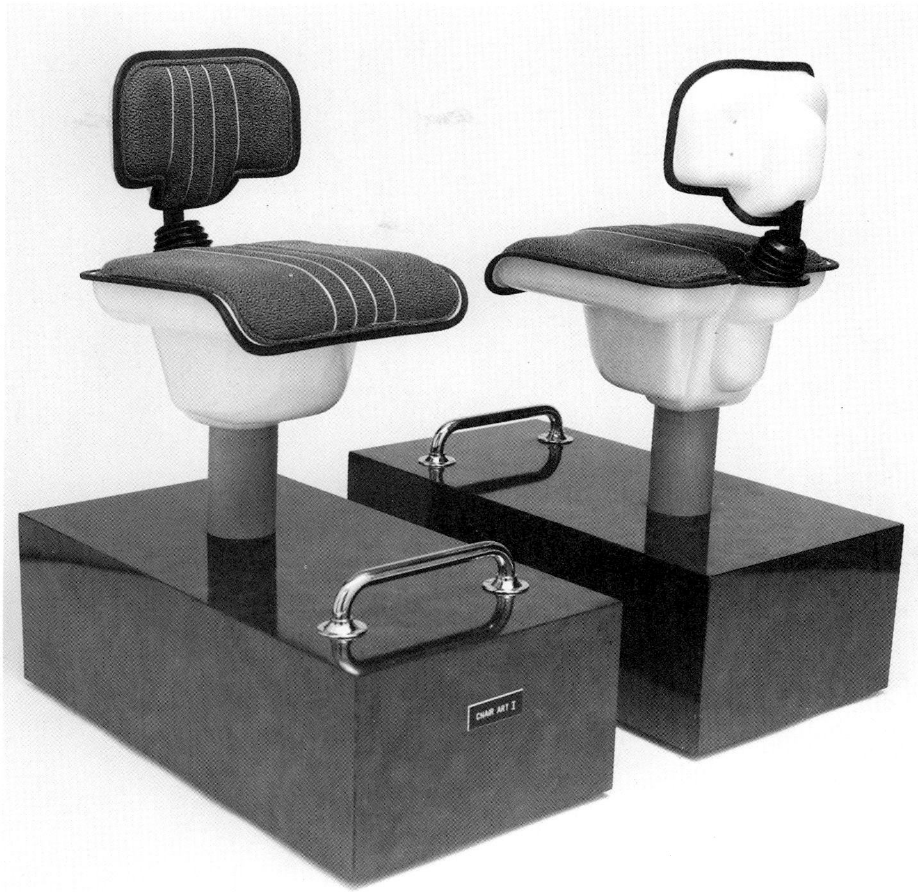

CHAIR ART I

Chair Art
1972/3. This began life as an ordinary draughting chair. The design evolved into a kind of museum piece, isolated from its interior function by its mounting on a mobile imitation marble plinth, complete with chrome door handles as implied foot rests. Chair art is 'an essay in the semantic vocabulary of materials'. It incorporates grey public transport upholstery; moulded pink surgical plastic; and black rubber trim, as used in automobile design.
Chair art is an exercise in furnishing imagery. It can be sat upon but it is not necessary or even particularly comfortable. Joint project, Geoff Hollington and Ben Kelly.

THE PHOTO KID

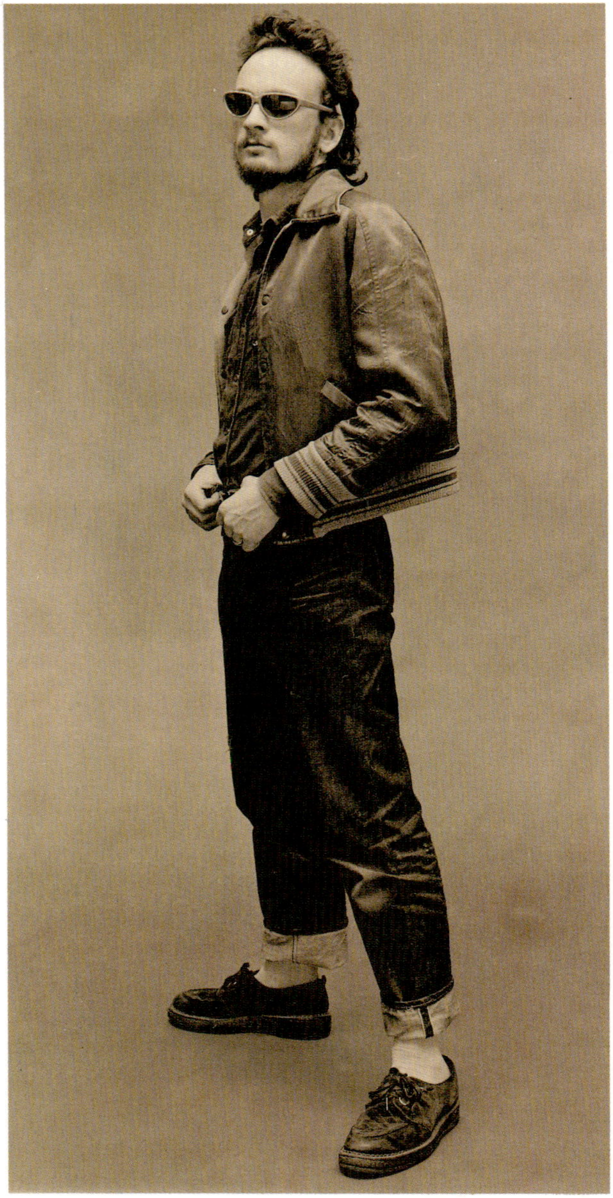

The Photo Kid
A.k.a Ben Kelly, 1972. The Photo Kid evolved as the result of disappointment and frustration with the majority of fellow students. It became necessary to adopt a different attitude, throw different poses and become detached from the crowd. An alter ego out to match Ziggy Stardust. A logical development of the Hockney peroxide, gold lamé, previous incarnation. The image could become product, artwork, whatever manifestation you cared to think of.

Metal Lined Cubicles
RCA Thesis, 1974. Produced out of necessity to document the Photo Kid's activities, human or otherwise, encouraged by such luminaries as Dickie Chopping and Reg Gadney. The written word became part of the creative process. The document required protection. The etched steel cover fulfilled this requirement. The steel cover was later to be appropriated by colleague Peter Saville for the cover of the single *Love will tear us apart* by Joy Division. The Factory connection was sealed.

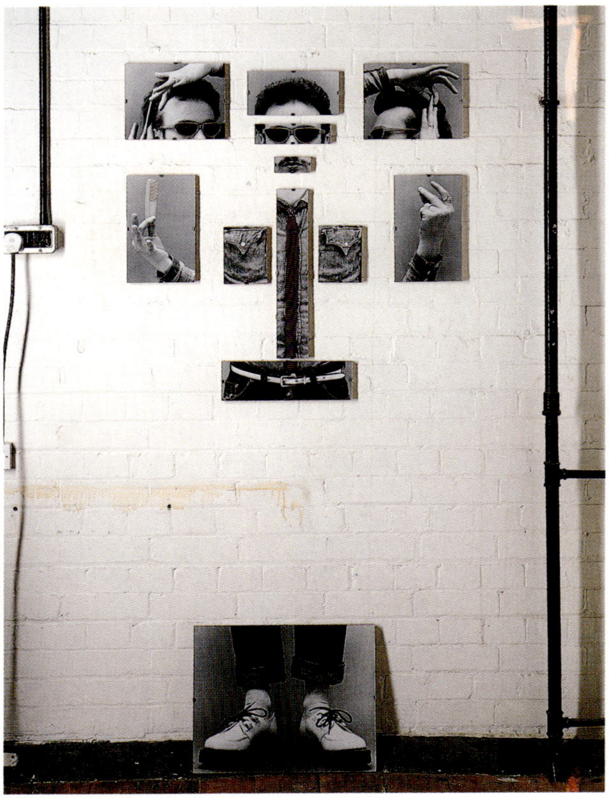

I AM THE PHOTO KID. I follow images. I am The Image Maker. I create images.
I am about images and images are what I am about. I take photos with my eyes.
I develop the photos in my mind. The photos are of images and they are images.
I am a camera in disguise. I caught a pair of shoes as they fell off the moon.
I pick my possessions from the street. I furnish my rooms from the city. My mind also.
I am an alien to the city. I pick up what I find.
I observe the territories the people create.
I see houses between the streets. I see shops punctuating the houses.
I see people living in the houses. I see the people passing over money for possessions.
I dance around. I pick up another apple which has fallen.
I shake another cigarette from the machine. I stand my feet in ice cubes.
I hear sirens wailing. The traffic stops. I take another picture.
I am approached by a man. He is covered in identity cards. He takes my picture.
I hear him say to me words of many meanings. City talk. Lights change to green.
I move on to another location. I begin to project another identity.
I begin to operate at a different level. I shed my former skin. I adopt a new pose.
I climbed up the wall of early morning light. I performed various inhuman activities.
I touch the keys to many questions. I enter the vault at the city centre.
I am close to the answer to the question of my present identity. I peel off layers.
I feel a cold wind blow across. I turn my face into the wind. I hear a solo single.
I hear a solo single singing in the wind. The sound wafts across.
I
I AM
I AM THE
I AM THE PHOTO
I AM THE PHOTO KID.

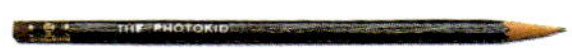

Ben Kelly

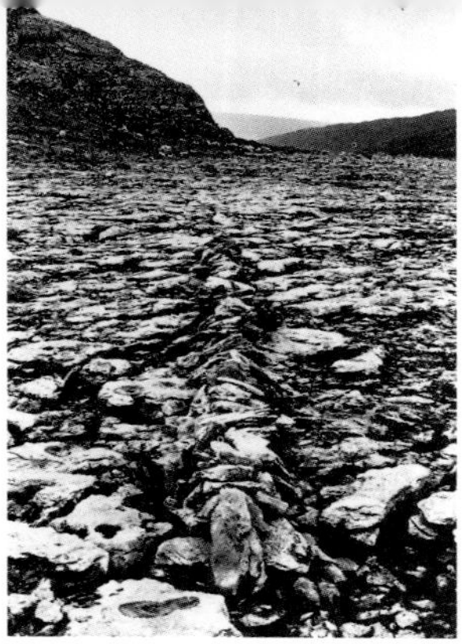

1

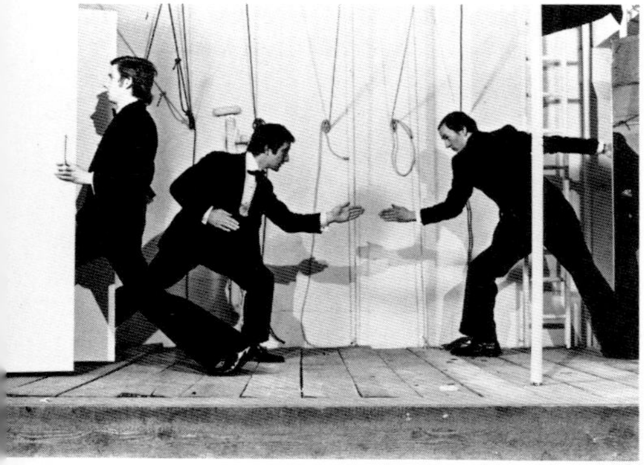

2

3

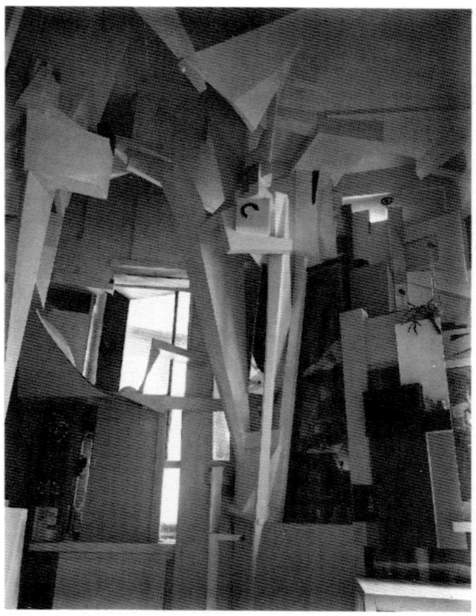

At the end of the sixties and the beginning of the seventies, the climate and direction for design in Britain could have gone in any number of directions which is exactly what it did. The King's Road, LSD and the Top Twenty helped to form attitudes towards visual awareness with an atom-splitting devastation.

Around 1967–70, I cannot recall many influences coming directly from the discipline of interior design itself. Perhaps Max Clendinning with his 'look no corners' soft environments in primary colours with the odd dash of silver. On the other side of the Atlantic, Andy Warhol's Factory: all silver walls, silver ceilings, silver cushions and minimal movies. Kenneth Anger's movies; soft and brutal, black and white, exaggerated colour, exaggerated everything. Captain Beefheart's 'soft and bulbous' *Trout Mask Replica.* They were all to do with attitude. In an age of confusion, history was out of the window.

Closer to home the more interesting ideas were coming from artists who pushed the boundaries into territories previously uncharted either by artists or designers. It seemed unnecessary to possess the actual skills or natural ability required to produce a work of art in the conventionally accepted form. Richard Long took a walk up a mountain and stretched out a line of stones, *A Line in Ireland*, 1974,[1] Barry Flanagan filled sacks with sand and Bruce McLean posed in a *Nice Style, The World's First Pose Band*.[2] One wondered whether these attitudes could find their way into interior design.

Kurt Schwitters' 1923 *Merzbau*,[3] a huge abstract grotto in which floor, walls and ceiling were joined by a labyrinth of struts, was Schwitters' response to the Constructivist idea of 'total environment'. A work which defied cataloguing or labelling, which could embrace any form but was actually a part of the environment. An inspirational set piece.

To pursue similar goals you must have sympathetic clients to indulge in the activity of looking for a style of self-expression. This is not an easy road.

To design is to communicate. Communication through language allows us to go about our daily lives. The language of design contains the same highs and lows as in communication through words. The juxtaposition of ideas in verbal or written form can cause excitement, stimulate thought, shock, please, or none of these. It seems a special moment when design achieves the same highs as language and literature. This is the space the artist occupies, uncluttered by the necessity to conform and answer problems.

John Miller

The objective of the Environmental Design School at the RCA from the early seventies to the early eighties was to bring together architecture and interior design. Two specialisms which should sustain each other but had grown apart, to their mutual disadvantage. The distinction between them being one of scale rather than substance. Ben's year was one of the first to confront this development and he and his contemporaries brought their own expectations to the course, challenging its intentions and putting the staff on its mettle.

The issues that engaged Ben at the Royal College are still alive fifteen years later in projects like the DRY201 bar where the piracy or transposition of elements originally intended for other purposes are juxtaposed with as-found surfaces, the spaces so formed avoid the merely 'sugary', are uncompromisingly tough to be softened only by the animation of the crowd.

Sir Hugh and Margaret Casson

The Royal College of Art

Shortly after the Festival of Britain, Robin Darwin invited us both to set up the first postgraduate School of Interior Design in the country. Robin invited people to start new departments not because they were the appropriate specialists but because he respected their approach to design and teaching and he enjoyed their company.

As the first Interior Design course in the country we faced enormous problems. Opposition came from the RIBA who still saw interior designers as decorators and as kind of pastry cooks or milliners. They saw them also as a threat and in this they have been proved right, as professional interior designers are beginning to move quite heavily into architecture.

Interior design is mostly short-term stuff but it had the flavour of theatre of fashion and of high-spirited impermanence. But although we set about trying to persuade the RIBA to recognise the activity as worthy of study they would not have any of it and it was only when John Miller put in a large architectural component that it was eventually recognised. One tricky problem we faced initially was that there were no schools of interior design from which to recruit our students into a postgraduate department. We looked not so much for architecture students but for people who showed a talent for ideas and three dimensional thinking. We made some mistakes but such was the talent and energy around that we had many successes.

By the time Ben and Geoff came to the college things had moved on a bit and the course had become more structured. These two were the advance guard for the next stage. They were obvious rebels. Geoff came from a conventional industrial design background but Ben was more of a generalist and an obvious maverick. They formed a marvellous partnership. They were the first and most welcome swallows of dissent bitterly resenting any attempt to imprison them and finding it impossible to identify with the T-square.

Ben and Geoff opened many new doors. In due course many of our students followed them into that land of pun, the fast track and the witty. They saw the point of the short term visual wisecrack.

Now that everything from toasters to marriages is regarded as inevitably short-term the swing back to more reassuring solutions begun by our department has a more rigorous flavour. But the high jinks of the sixties, seventies and early eighties have left their mark. Ben and Geoff were amongst those who sharpened everybody's wits and pencils and never forgot to be professionals.

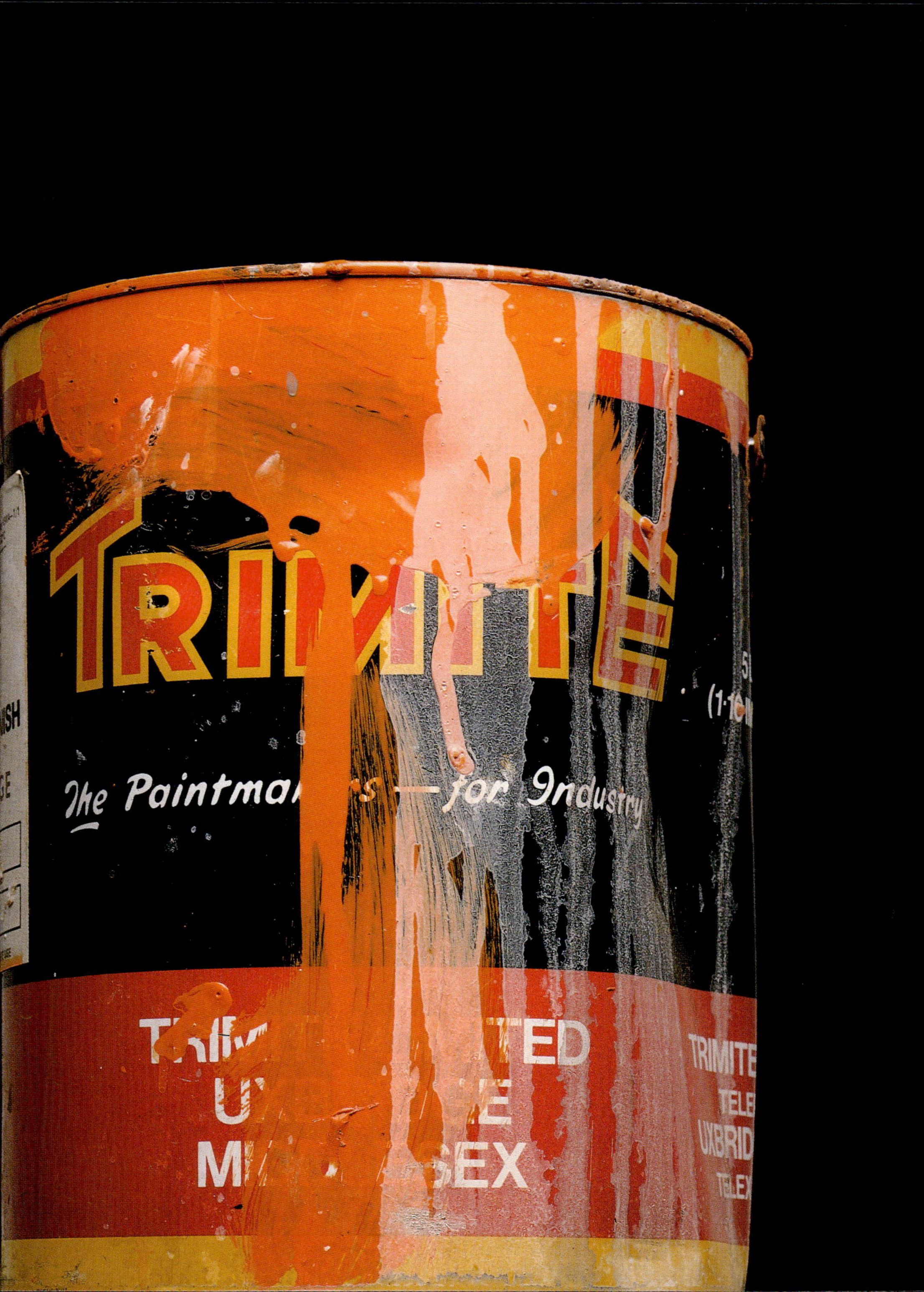

for Industry
TRIMITE

2 INTERNATIONAL ORANGE

Paul Howie

Ben Kelly is an English interior designer whose work, created with unorthodox brilliance and presented with enthusiasm and anxiety, falls into none of the accepted categories of design. I live and work in environments created by this man.

Now just past forty he is a man of singular appearance, his face presenting bewilderment, amazement, humour, exasperation, creativity, joy, hedonism and a searching spirit within the space of a two-minute conversation.

Of average height, his hair reluctantly thinning, clad in close-fitting monochrome clothes often relieved by geometrical design, Ben's persona is that of the questing yeoman artist puzzled by his status in life. He longs for his rightful acclaim, long overdue, which will provide him with the continued opportunities to satisfy his creative needs. I have argued and caroused with Ben for fifteen years. He is one of my best friends.

I first met Ben and his consort, clothes designer Chrissie Walsh at my Fulham Road menswear shop in 1974. Both were fresh from the RCA and eager to put their ideas into action. Each continues to exert beneficial influence on the other. Both have remained true to their creative beliefs.

Ted Walters

He found the client and then by pure chance met me. The most important issue in our working relationship was the period in time we started working together. At the time of our meeting, a shop-fitting aesthetic did not exist as it does today. At the time the important thing was the object being displayed and not the environment.

The Howie shop in 1976 developed the idea of the environment being as important as the product on the shelf, possibly to the extreme that the environment became the object. It was a great shock to me to see that Ben had made the designed environment more prominent, more important than the goods for sale. It was also a shock to me when I discovered what Ben was trying to do. He wanted to bring art into the world of Interior design and specifically the fashion retail industry. His problem was finding someone who understood what he was trying to achieve and was capable of making it.

As a student studying sculpture at St Martins I had approached art functionally, and was interested in minimalism and raw materials. His work appealed to me because it was reductionist, uncompromising and superficially naïve. I was thrown in at the deep end with the demands of Ben's designs. I became obsessed with achieving his aesthetic aims.

Things which the tradesmen considered insignificant became critical. Through my involvement with sculpture, my concern was with the object, in translating the drawings into reality I became fascinated as Ben was by the environment inhabited by the object.

My empathy with Ben and sympathy with his aesthetic goals expedited the entire process from concept to reality. It has been my task to interpret drawings, handle materials and modify the habitual behaviour of tradesmen, in order to ultimately realise the conception of a considerable number of Ben Kelly's projects since the Howie shop. In undertaking this work over the years I have realised what an invaluable asset it was for me to have completed a sculpture course, instilling in me an ability to consider the manipulation of the normal parameters of everyday environments (i.e. shops, clubs, bathrooms) and the non-contextual use of materials.

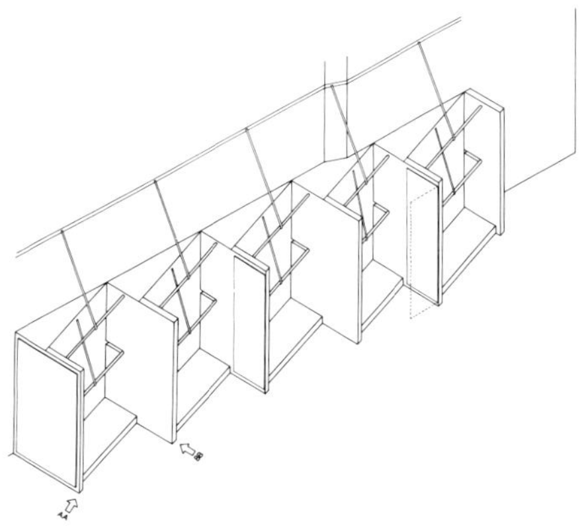

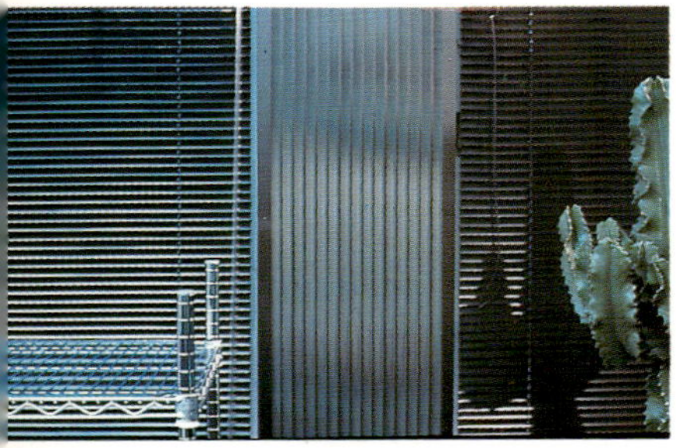

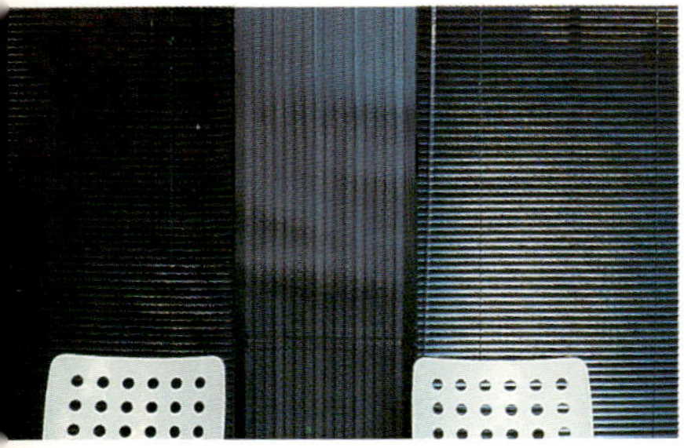

Dereta Showroom
1979/80. Designed to house clothing collections by Paul Howie, entitled 'Paul Howie at Dereta. Clothes for the Modern Woman'. The scheme furnished one small room and enabled buyers to view models wearing the collections. Hans Coray silver aluminium chairs are set in front of black perforated steel panels. Eileen Gray Bibendum chairs were used to offer comfort to the buyers. The circular mirror was mounted on a wall covered in random Letraset letters, spelling the name of the designer and the showroom.

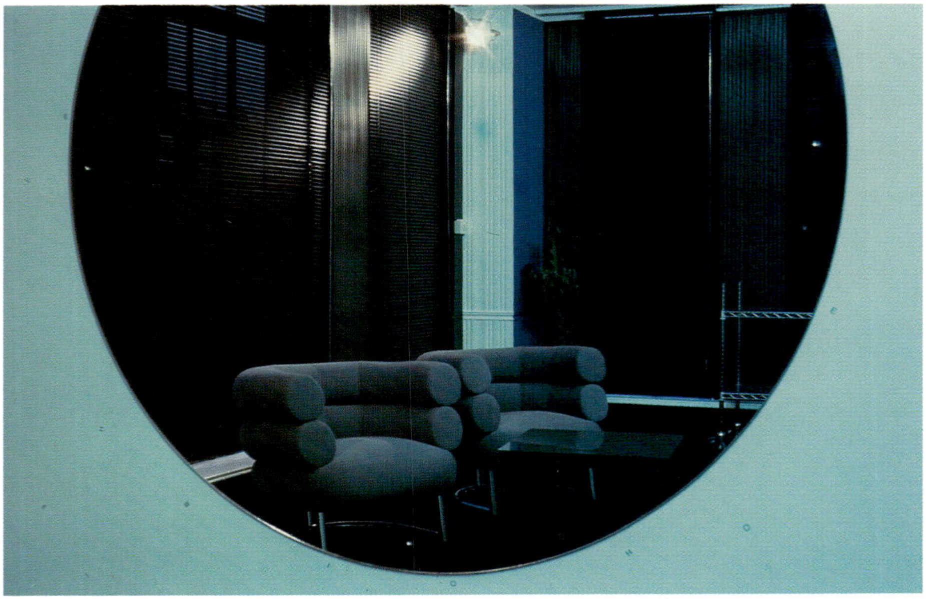

Howie

Clothes shop, Covent Garden 1977. The Howie shop was my first solo commission. It came at a time when London seemed to be going through a period of transition in fashion and design. It proved to be an important commission. It allowed me to experiment and make a different statement about the art of fashion retail, and its possibilities. The shop, commissioned by Lynne Franks and Paul Howie started life as 'Mrs. Howie' and became 'Howie' when the basement opened up to sell menswear.

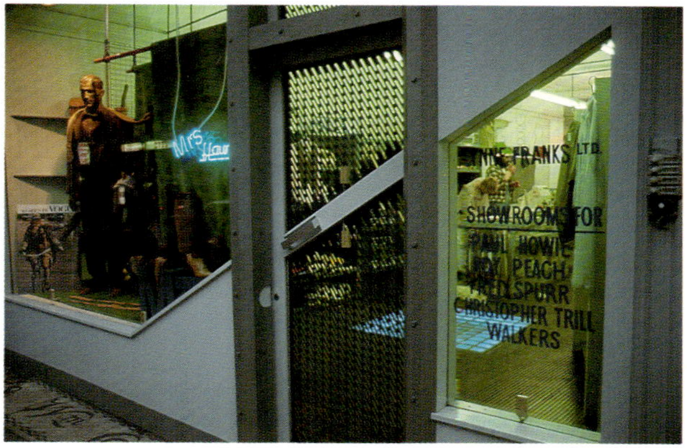

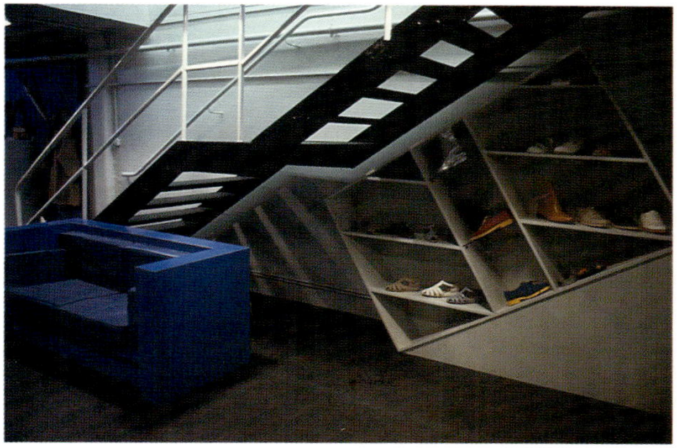

It was my first opportunity to experiment with materials and objects in a retail environment. My fascination with industrial materials resulted in the use of black ribbed rubber heavy-duty flooring; galvanised Dexion; galvanised Kee Klamp tubing with epoxy blue coated fittings; galvanised wire mesh; off-the-peg factory storage bins and steel shelving. Yachting fittings were adapted for window displays, and specially spliced nylon rope was used to support analine-dyed

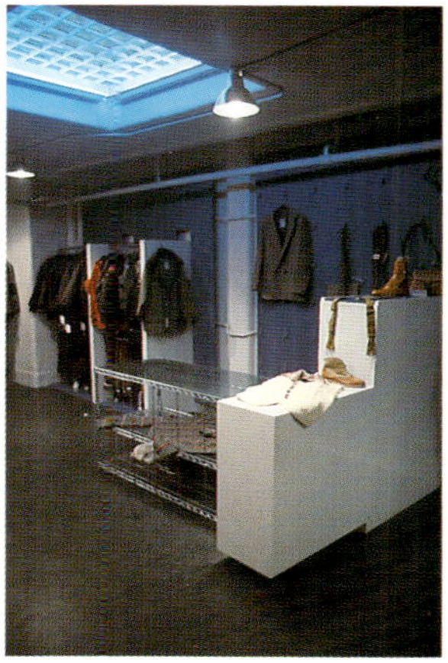

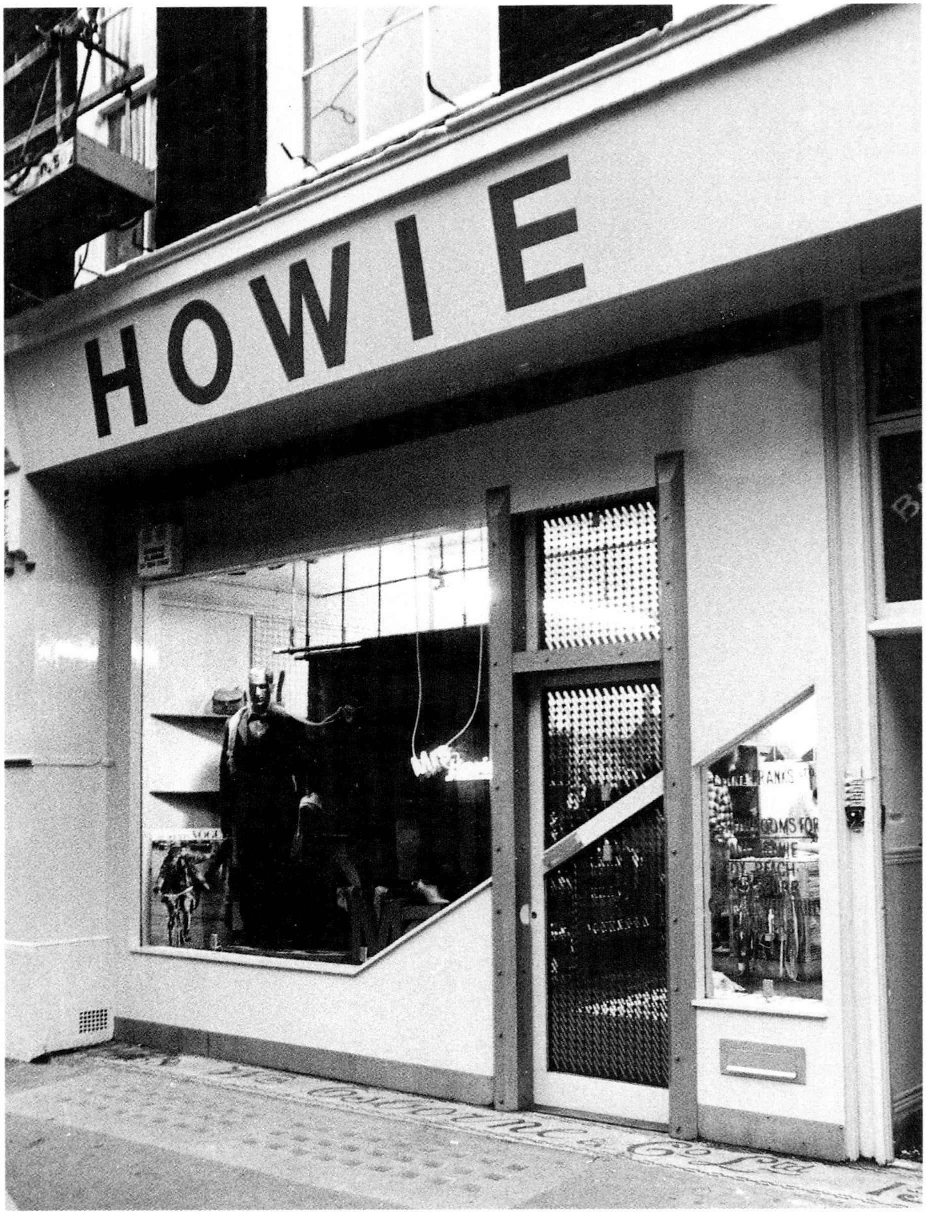

brightly-coloured, wooden hanging rails. Three light fittings were specially designed in red, blue and green anodised aluminium with folded shades. These were bolted onto a perspex spine with clear plastic laboratory tubing carrying the stripped live, neutral and earth wires through holes in the perspex. They hung over the galvanised Dexion and polished plate Georgian wire glass counter. Industrial fluorescent tube system lighting hung on black steel conduits, supplemented with photographic reflectors, provided the main lighting. Perforated steel panels with a Hammerite finish were inset into the glazed door panels. These were to provide the basis for my collaboration with Peter Saville on the Orchestral Manœuvres' perforated sleeve, and ultimately my connection with Factory Records.

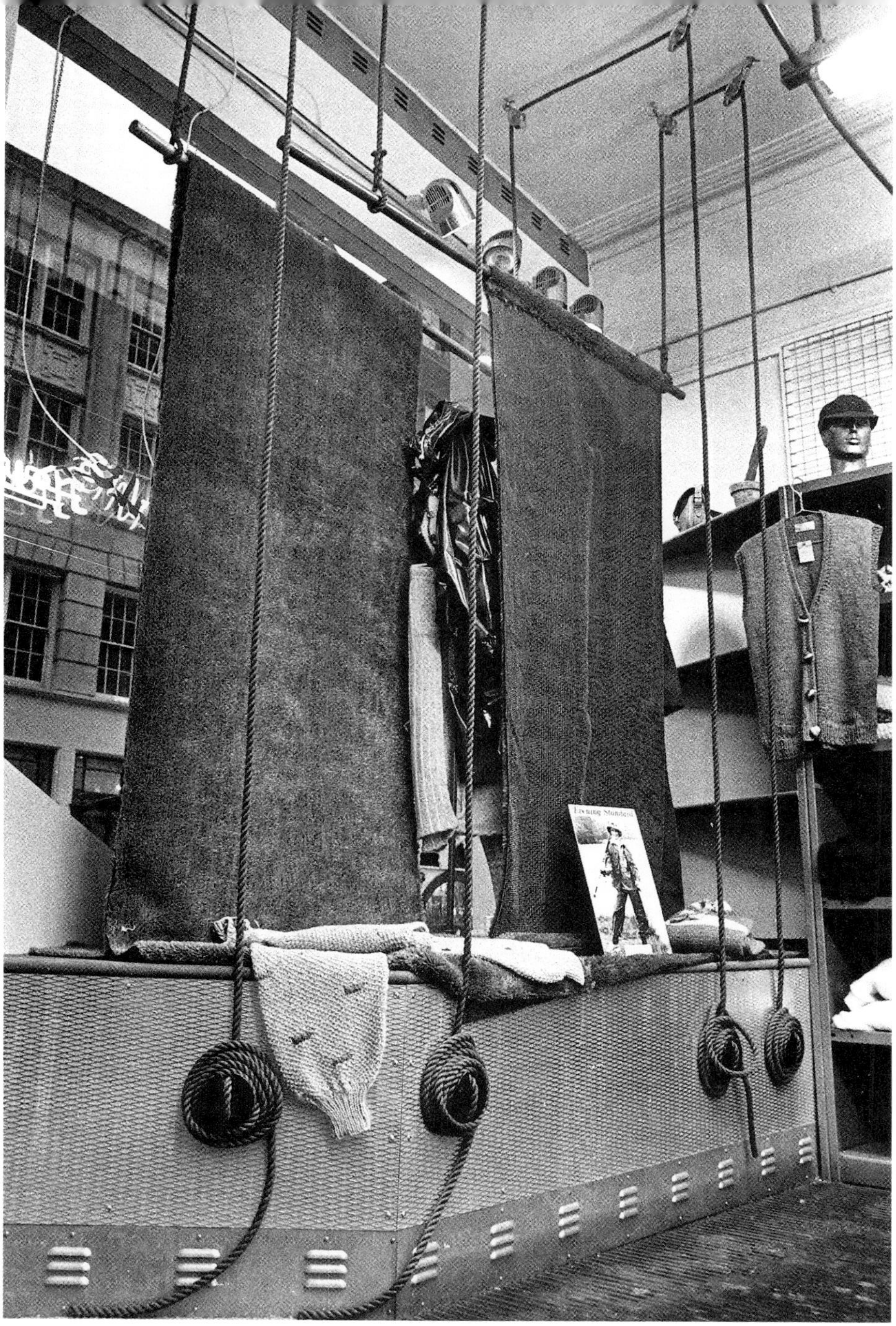

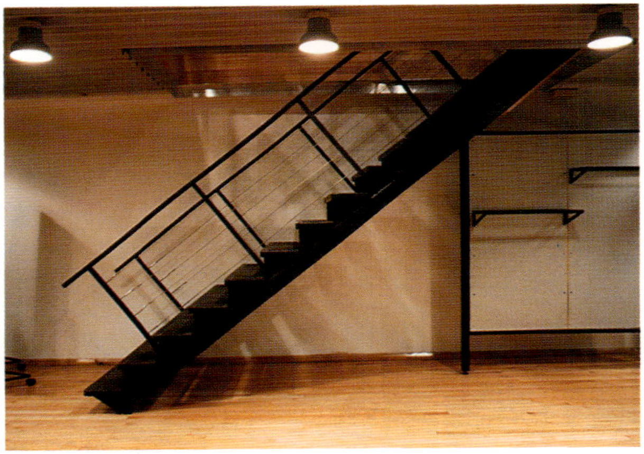

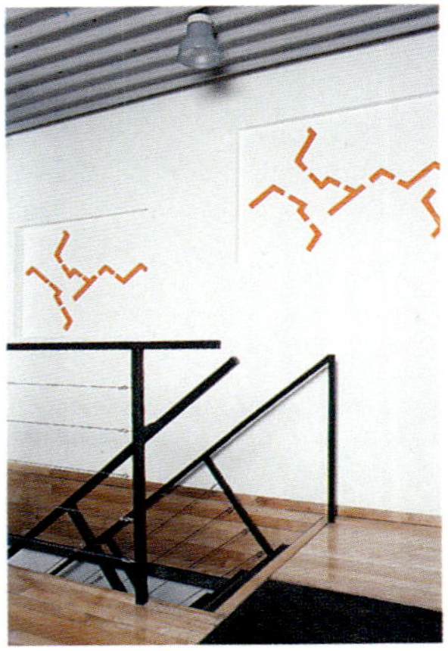

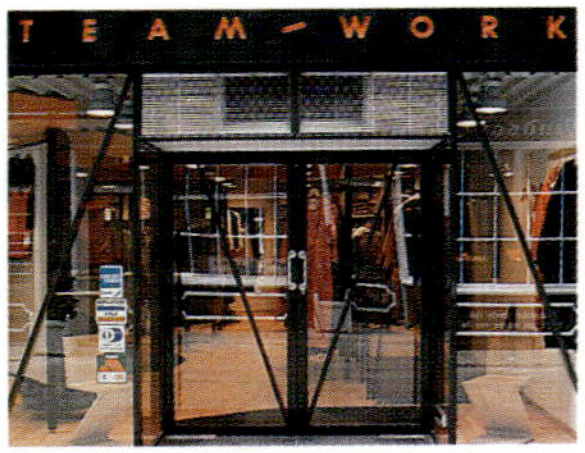

Teamwork
Clothes shop, 1980. The brief was to provide the shop with an overall identity but to indicate eight separate fashion concessions on two floors. I wanted to provide the separation more by implication than by physical separation. Frank Gehry's Mid- Atlantic Toyota offices provided a clue through the use of overhead angular beam devices which crashed through the layout in a random fashion, offering an implied structure. I developed a system of floating, hard-edged, zig-zag boxes which clung to the industrial profiled-steel ceiling. The high-gloss structures gave the necessary separation to the plan form by implication. They also supported a shelving and hanging-rail system for each concession. The staircase connecting the two floors was a major element in the scheme. We tried to make the stair integral with the scheme by using similar materials and structural elements.

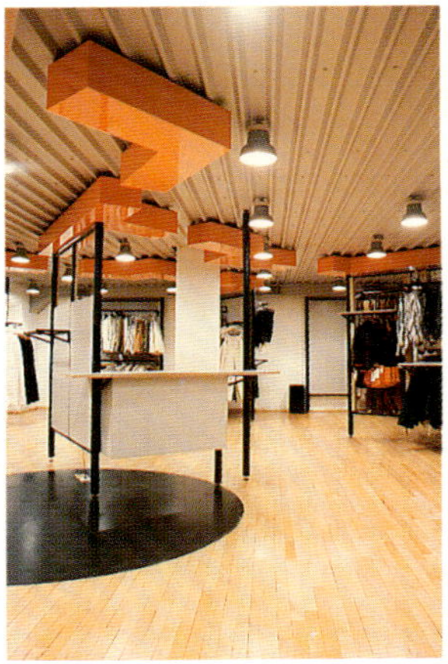

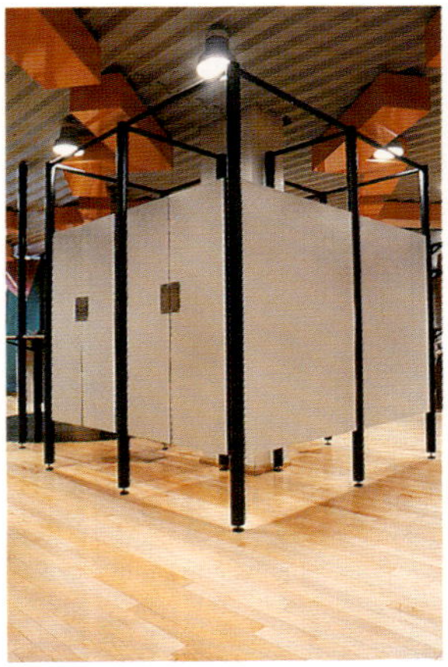

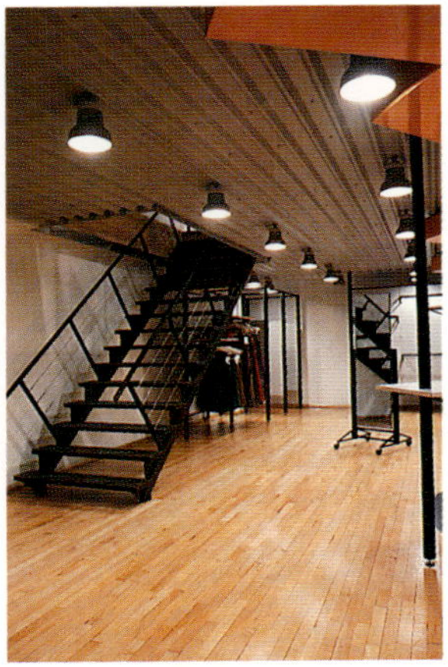

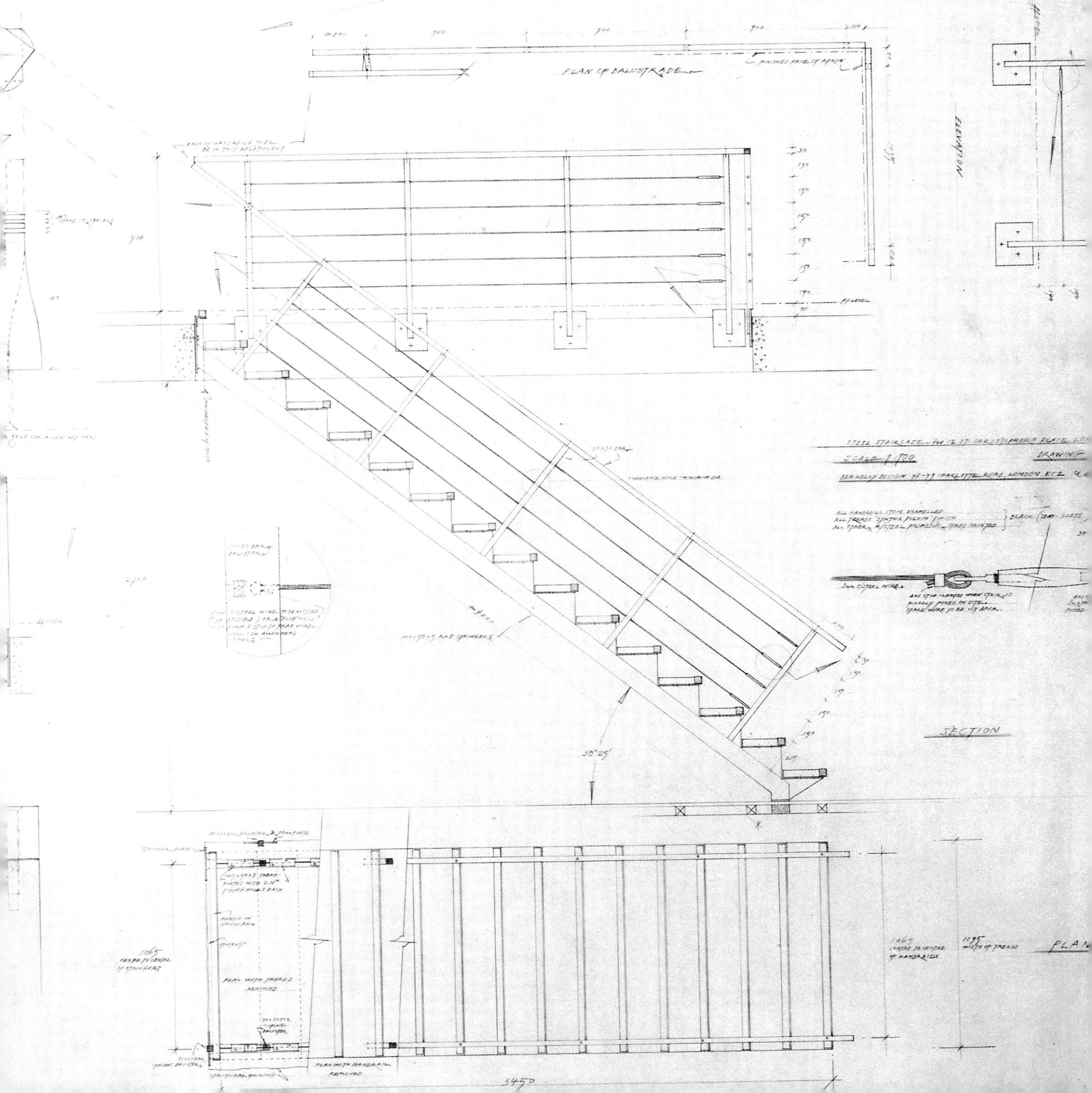
PLAN OF BALUSTRADE
ELEVATION
SECTION
PLAN
SCALE 1:100
DRAWING
ALL HANDRAILS STOVE ENAMELLED
ALL TREADS 'SYNTHA PULVIN' FINISH
ALL OTHER M/STEEL PRIMED & SPRAY PAINTED
BLACK (SEMI-GLOSS
3mm S/STEEL WIRE
SPARE WIRE TO BE CUT BACK.
100×50×5 RHS STRINGERS
30×30 BAR
FF LEVEL
38°25'
3450
1065
1195
WIDTH OF TREADS
PLAN WITH TREADS REMOVED
PLAN WITH HANDRAIL REMOVED
900
150

Fred Scott

Like the common cold, interior design, despite its prevalence, is lacking in definition. Recently, a designer suggested there was no such thing, or if examined, it would be found to be totally subsumed by architecture. The opposite temptation therefore is to attempt to describe interior design in terms of what architecture is not, or rather to ascertain in which ways it is distinct from architecture. In terms of the geography of human effort, it lies somewhere between architecture and set design, more artistic than one, less dramatic than the other.

Recent architectural theories have emphasised the timeless quality of buildings, especially in the relationship with the city. Regarding true architecture as essentially unchanging, like a rock, over which at different times different uses will wash.

Architecture is timeless; interior design is temporal. Lack of interest in temporal qualities weakens the architect's attachment to other previously important considerations. For instance, interest in the role of the client, and more generally, interest in most of the programmes with which today they are likely to be presented. The latter echoes the reaction against the commitment to a social programme which was a characteristic of the previous generation.

The new theories dictate a stance which is removed from such matters. In the replacement of Parker Morris with poetics, an air of suspension has permeated architectural vision, frozen banners in a departed wind. The interior designer can afford no such other worldliness. In his world the role of the client is paramount, and also whereas most clients can be relied upon to understand area, there are a few that will understand space. The architect tends to dream his production. The designer however is always aware of the client's hot breath and, like a striker in a game of football, or someone waking, he must struggle to make space in the face of intense distraction.

Other differences are clear in the approach to the work. For the interior designer there is no equivalent of a clear site; the least limiting of interior space with which the designer must contend is more conditioned than almost all sites with which the architect is presented. Consequently there is a different consciousness required of the interior designer in the approach to his or her work. It is provoked by this condition of fitting, of always working with and within existing structures. Because of this, a structured understanding of the host building is an essential preliminary to the consideration of any intervention. The understanding needs to be a common language derived from the actuality of the built form, a language which will allow a mental deconstruction, informing the physical alterations. It requires of the designer a thoughtful stripping back of the host building. An understanding must be reached which is material, spatial and cultural.

Through an intellectual approach, the designer may establish his correct standing between the extremes of limp mimicry and ill-mannered outlandishness, and by this, establish a basis for the ensuing rules of intervention. Classifying such rules is beyond the ambitions of this piece, except to say that the designer needs to realise that sometimes he will be more accomplished than the original author of the building and similarly sometimes will be able to clarify by his intervention the original architectural intentions, and in so doing, in some ways, to complete the building with which he is working.

The relationship between style and way of life is the matrix within which the designer operates; interior design is essentially the orchestration of new life in old buildings. Interior design establishes its relationship with architecture by involvement in space-making and fuses this relationship in a common interest in the plan.

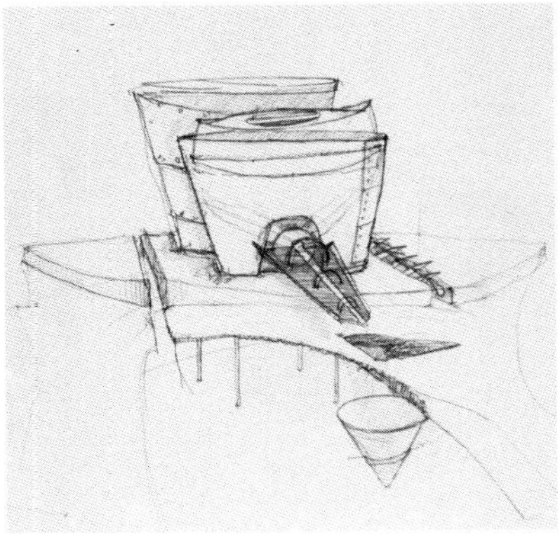

Sarah Dallas Studio
Mill conversion for knitwear company, 1984. Our clients approached us to convert an old wool mill into showrooms, offices, warehouse and design studio for their knitwear business. The scheme was carried out on two floors to a minimal budget. We developed a system of glazed steel frames, glass block, studwork and solid low wall partitions. These were set against the existing sandblasted timber beams and cast-iron columns which we painted different colours. We tried to create a semi-sculptural environment using relatively cheap and straightforward materials.

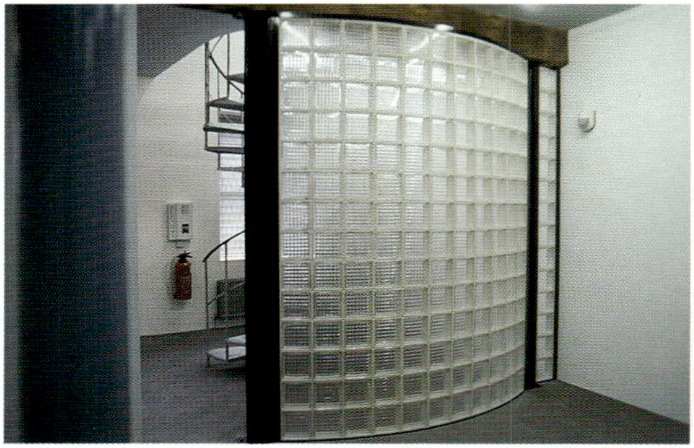

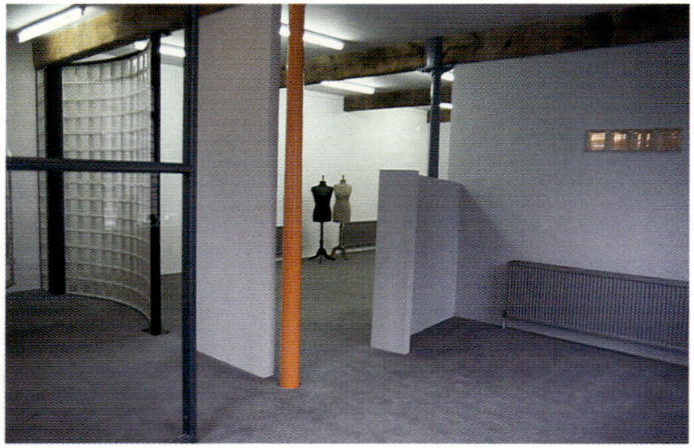

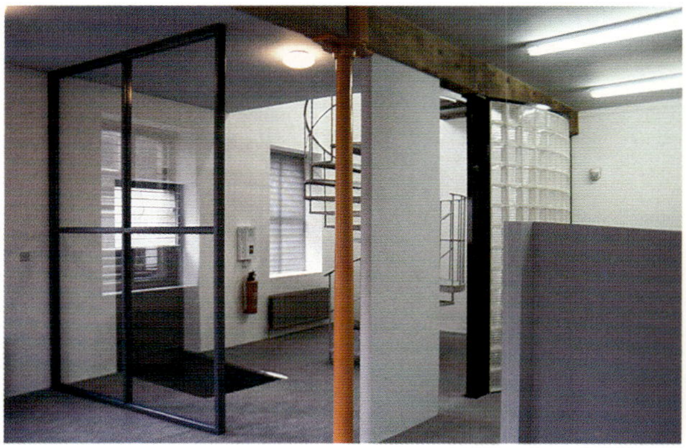

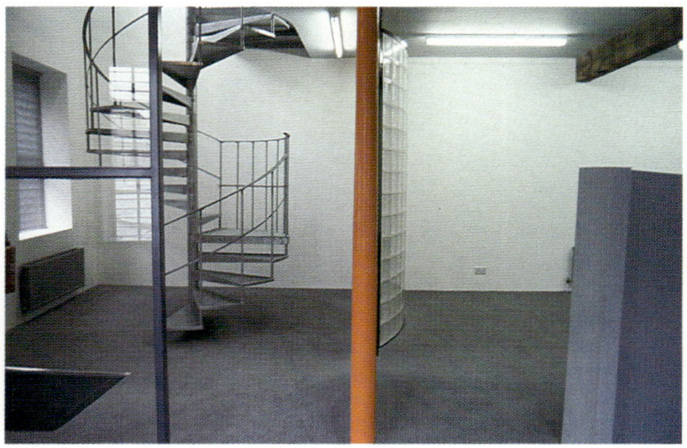

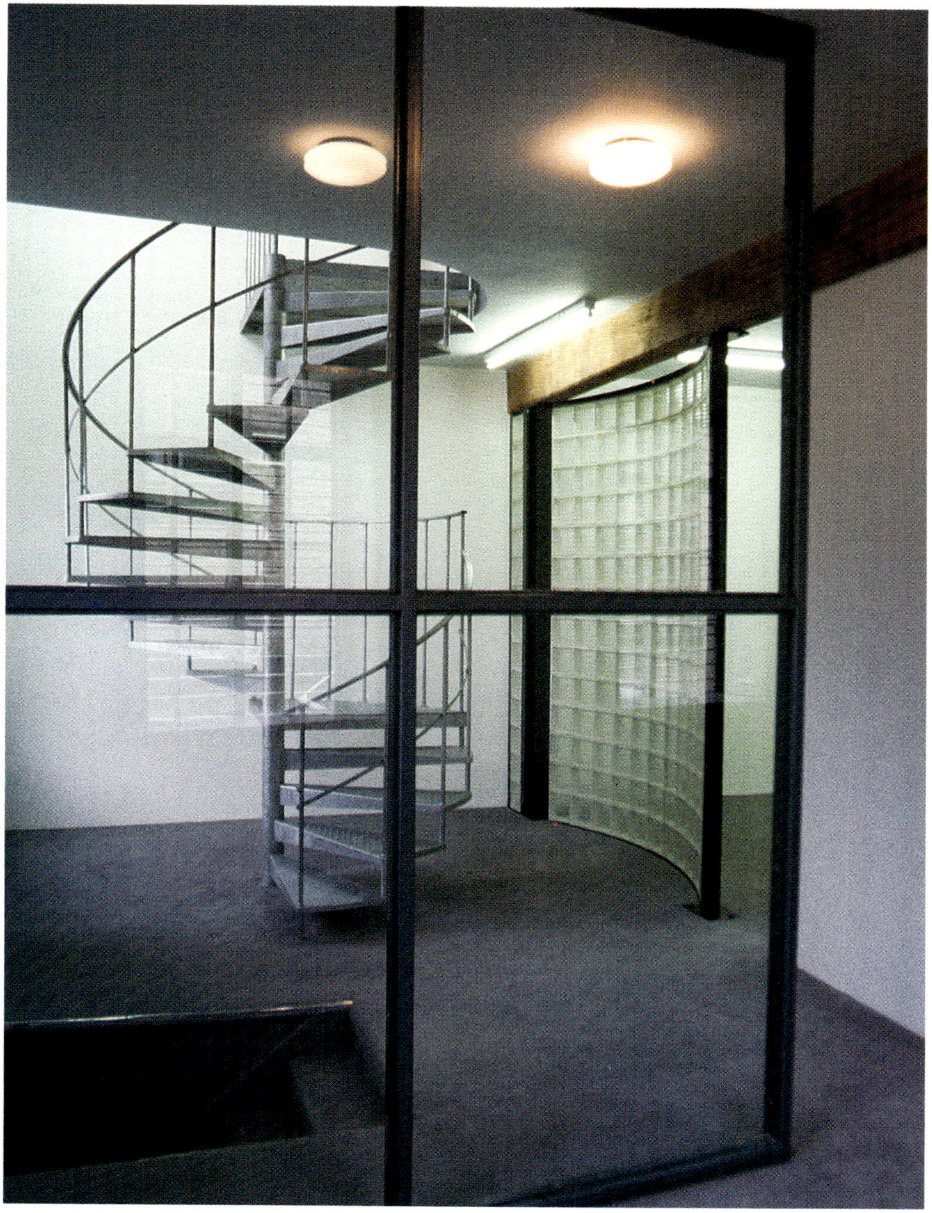

Keith Wainwright

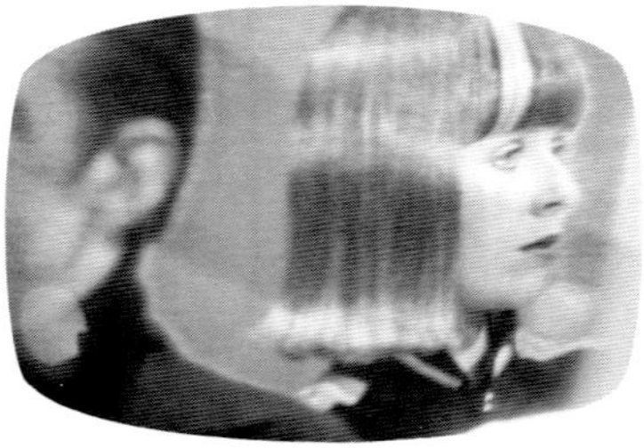

Keith Wainwright with his partner Leslie Russell own Smile, one of the best-known hairdressing teams in London. They describe Smile precisely as a shop and not a salon. It is an important distinction in terms of the design, because they wanted to shift the emphasis away from the traditional devices of an open salon.

I like Ben because he is a modernist

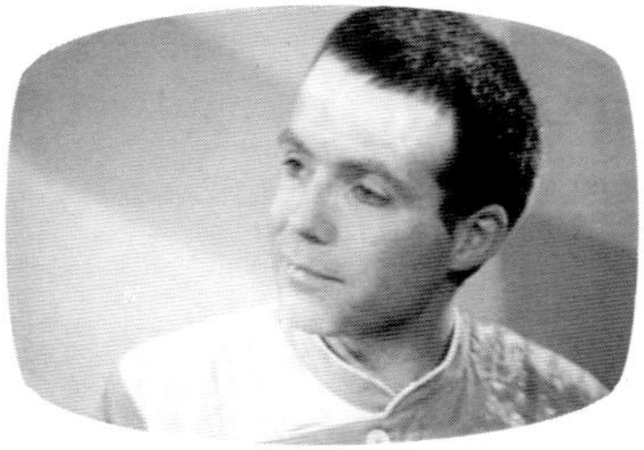

I had pioneered a move away from natural hair to Punk aggression using bleach and unnatural colours including scarlet red and brilliant orange. This encouraged the idea that at last you could own up to the activity of dyeing hair. We then attempted to get rid of the clichés associated with hairdressing salons of the decade. Our shared taste embraced hard uncompromising materials. Granite worktops and a Welsh slate floor were specified. When local planning officers turned down a proposal for horizontal glazing bars a more efficient solution was found in sandblasted glass bands. Natural daylight enters but passers-by are not invited to look in. Lit at night the façade becomes an illuminated formal image.

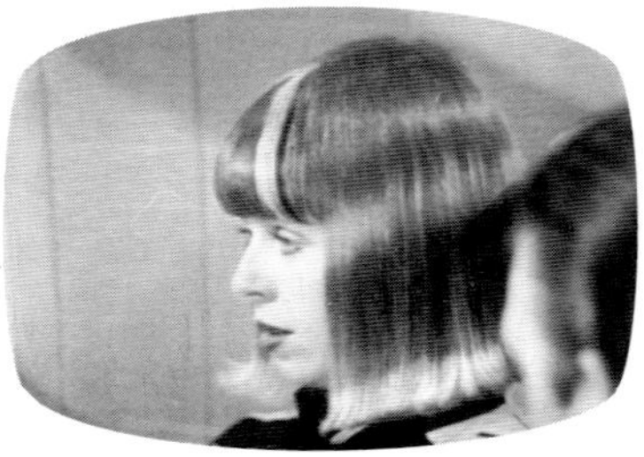

Ben Kelly

Hello Worlds End. A smile from Knightsbridge to the King's Road, number 434. Almost next door to the hallowed ground of Punkature, and the now-going-backwards clock.

This was to be a serious building conversion. Take the building apart from top to bottom. Put it back together with a mesh of new structural steelwork. Keep it hard-edged, soften it with materials, present a face to the street. A formal linear shopfront. Be careful not to allow too many points of reference. What happens inside? No one is too sure. Let's keep them guessing. Is it a bird or is it a plane? Across the void, concrete to slate. Through the airlock lobby. Large bands of light fall through the glass and down into the void. Hairstyles. Individual styling positions, no two identical, with a common language of materials and a shared identity. Circular mirrors, square mirrors, rectangular mirrors, recessed mirrors, projecting mirrors. Silver, gold and orange, the scrapheap of style. Smile, thank you. Have a nice day.

Smile
Hairdressing salon, 1983. Smile had existed as a successful hairdressing salon in Knightsbridge for several years. The owners decided to expand the operation to the King's Road where they purchased an old house with shop premises on ground-floor level. We were required to convert the floors above ground level into two self-contained flats and fit the hairdressing area with a beauty salon on ground and basement levels. To allow separate access to

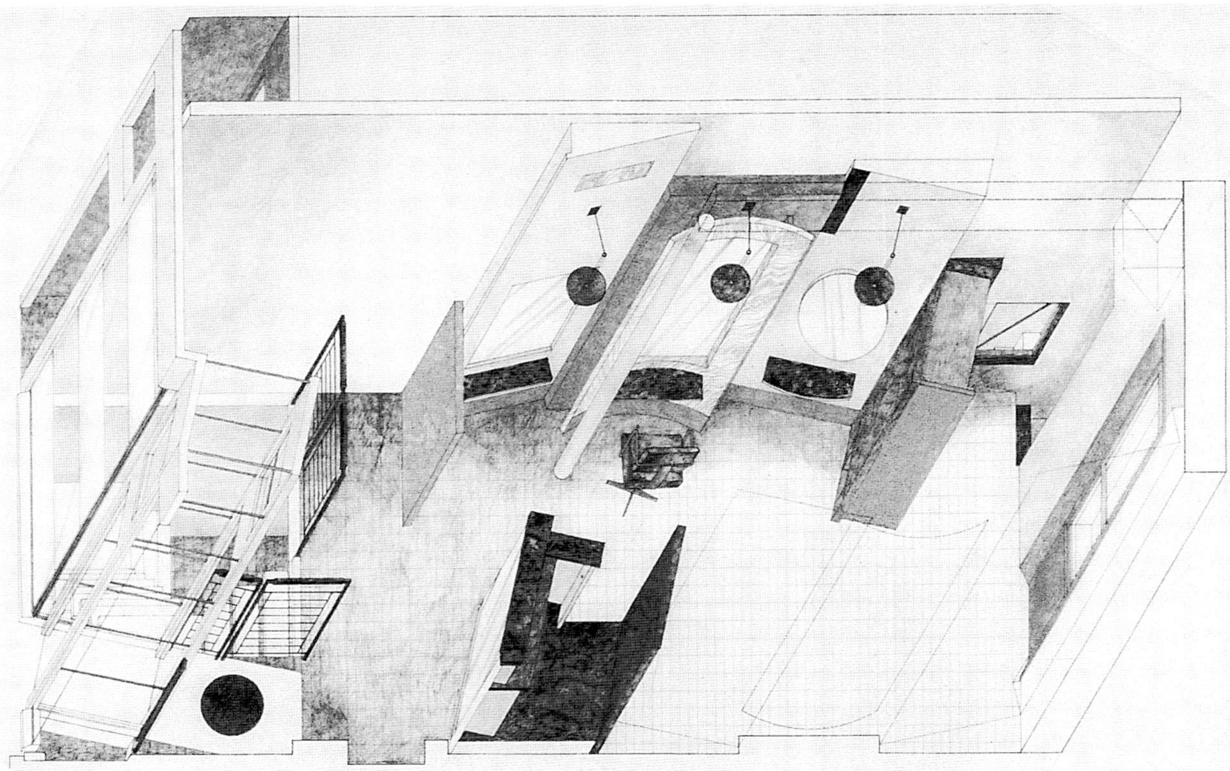

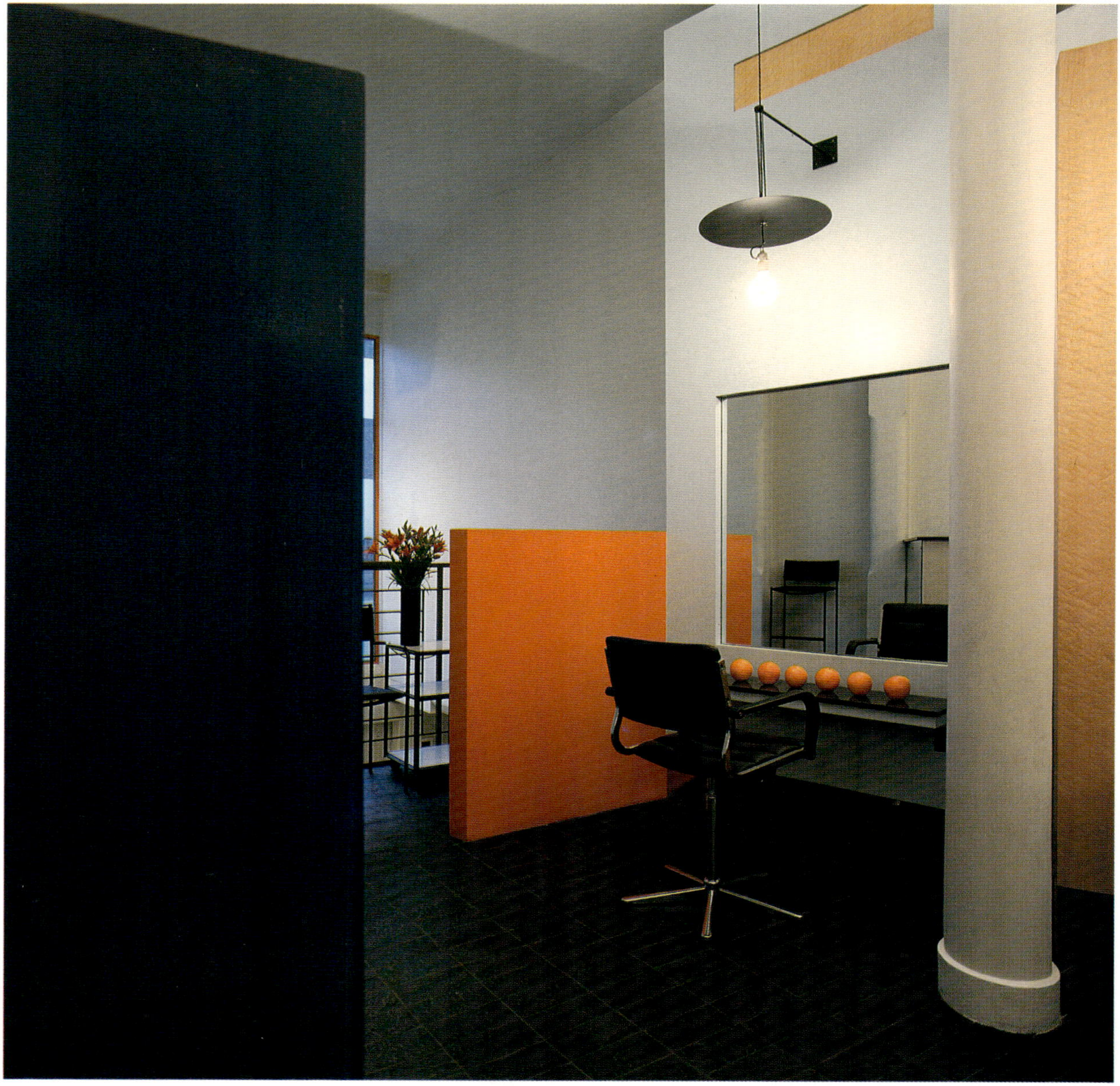

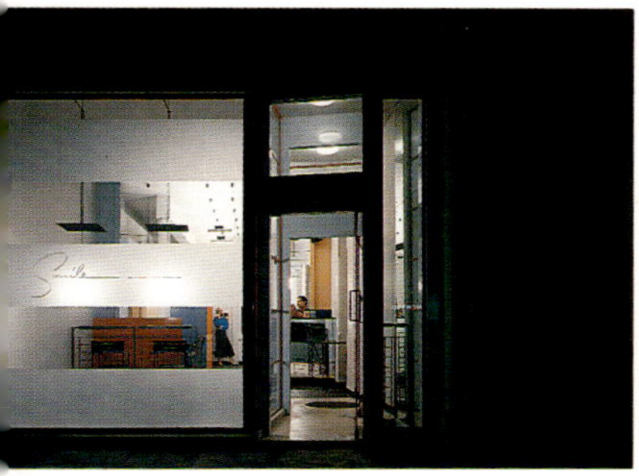

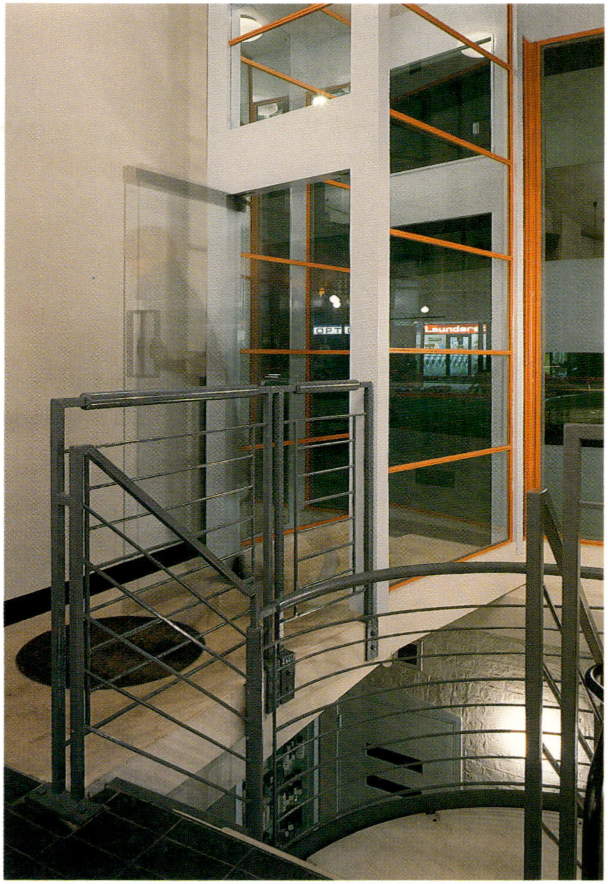

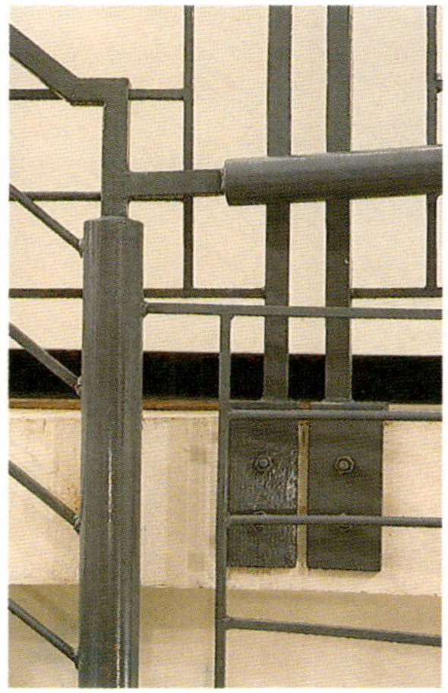

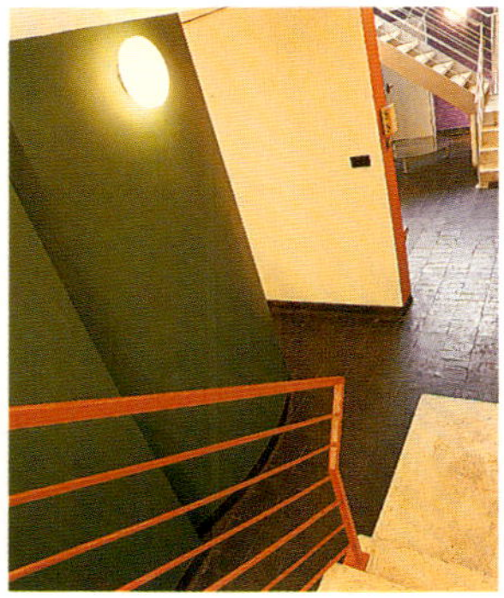

the flats, the ground-floor area became a narrow space. An early decision was to open up the front area and allow maximum daylight through the new shop front into the basement. This gave us the opportunity to drop the staircase into the void and create a sculptural link between the floors. By visually linking the two levels, the narrow space appeared to have a larger scale. We wanted to build an environment which readdressed the issues and functional requirements of hairdressing. With this in mind, we set about designing a scheme which looked as little like a hairdressing salon as possible.

Two staircases link the floors. A rear stair was constructed using in situ concrete, left as a 'natural' finish. The front stair in the void combined structural steel elements with pre-cast concrete treads. The main flight of the stair sits on an in situ landing. A pre-cast concrete 'bridge' allows access from the entrance across the void onto the main floor. A steel-framed glazed lobby sits on the bridge and links vertically with the staircase construction. The whole assembly is connected with the steel-framed shopfront.

The styling positions were developed through a geometry set out on plan. This allowed a series of curves and angles to become vertical surfaces which could support granite shelves and house different shaped mirrors. We then designed steel light fittings which hung above each styling position and unified the different geometries, materials and colours. A slate floor provided a functional and sympathetic surface for sweeping up the day's labour. Strong colours were used to offset the natural finishes, with the use of an industrial orange prompting one particular journalist to announce than 'Ben Kelly has rescued the colour orange from the scrap heap of style'. Sandra's use of gold on a rear window seemed a more appropriate colour for the description.

A few years after the salon opened, our clients felt it was time to re-decorate the interior. As designers, we did not want to lose the original æsthetic, but understood the practical requirements. Through using a series of bright colours, including purple as opposed to orange, we discovered that we had produced an environment which captured the spirit of 1989 – acieeed.

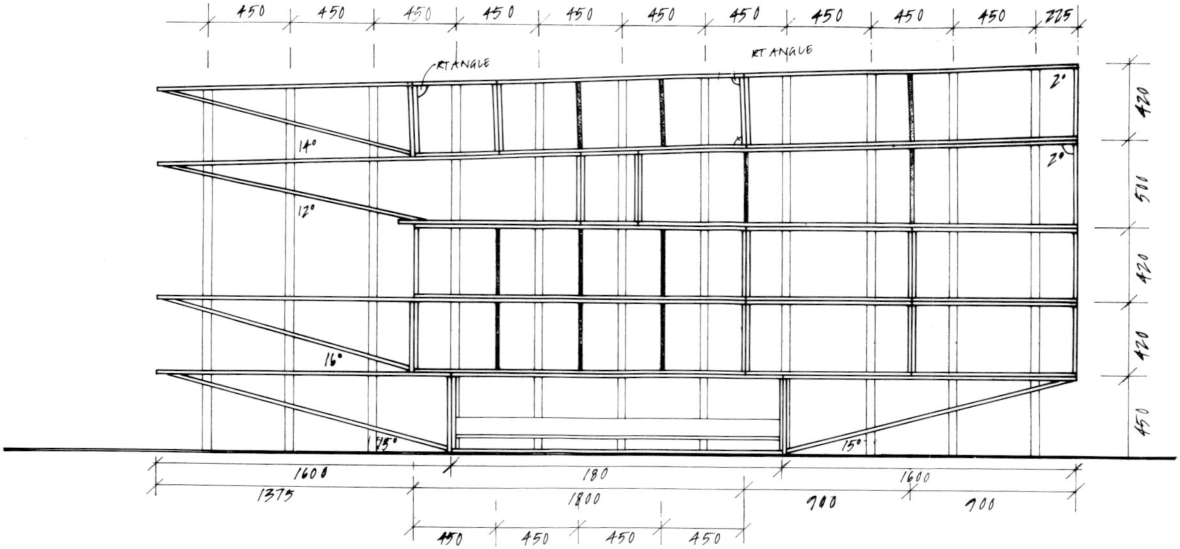

Pickwick Clothing
Clothes shop and headquarters building 1987–88. The company owns the Quincy and Jones shops.
For the Quincy shop on Floral Street, the client wanted to create a mini department store with suits on the first floor, shoes and casual wear in the basement, and with shirts and accessories on the ground floor. We decided it was necessary to keep the existing central staircase and work around it. As with the Quincy, Dean Street shop, the client decided to use an old shopfitting counter in a prominent position on the ground floor. Again, we stripped back to the original shell. The walls, steelwork and timber beams were sandblasted and sealed. Using Douglas fir, shelving units and changing cubicles were designed as free-standing elements. The main ground floor unit became known as 'junk shelving'.

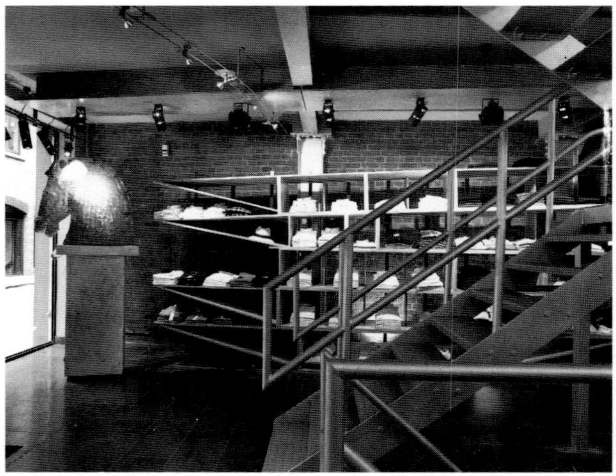

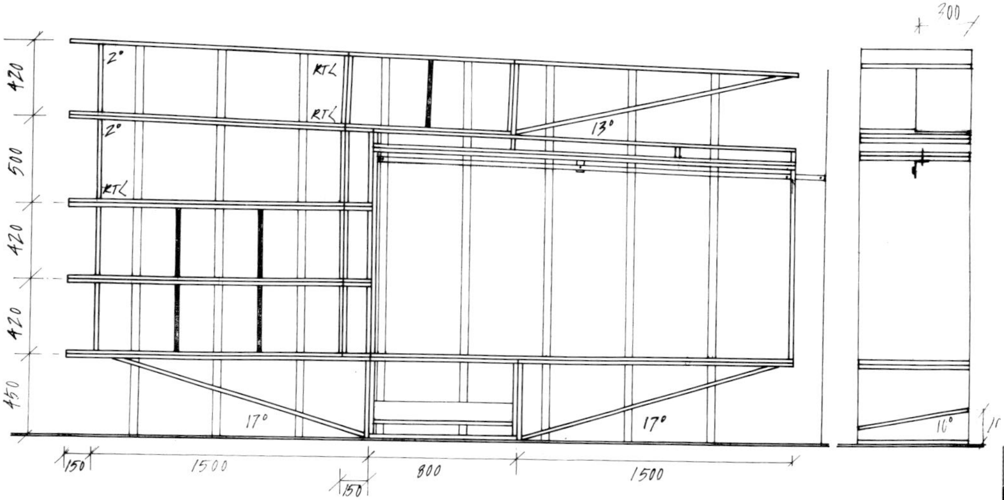

420
500
420
420
450
2°
2°
RTL
RTL
RTL
13°
17°
17°
10°
150
1500
150
800
1500
300

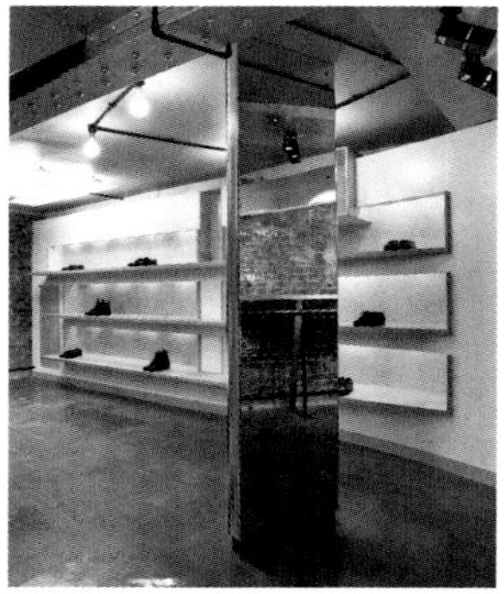

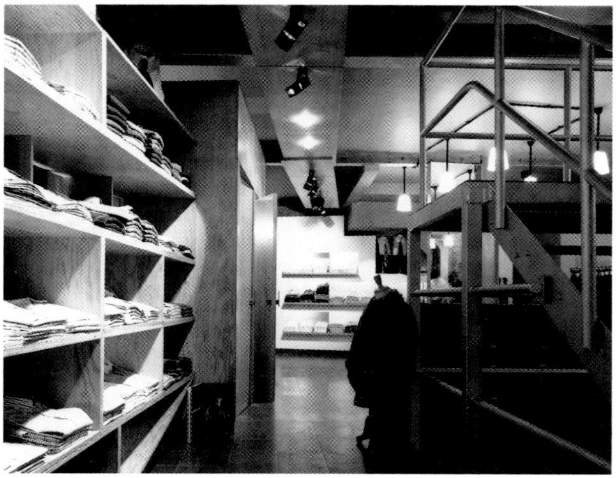

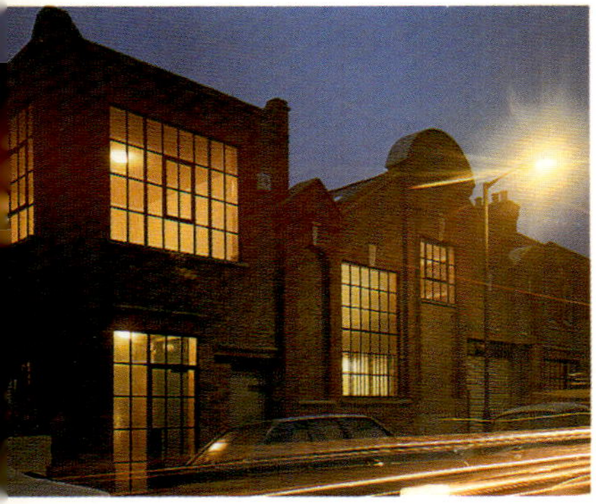

At Prairie Street the clients had purchased an old community hall which had to be converted into the company's headquarters building, combining offices, showroom and warehouse. Internally the building offered possibilities for two levels, with an upper level taking in the roof space. This allowed us to create a double-height office, linked by openings in the separating partitions to an upper office and landing. A new curved wall separated the double-height office from the loading bay, which was given direct access from the street into the warehouse. A roller shutter and sliding doors completely seal off the loading bay from the warehouse and the street. The basic idea of the scheme was to provide practical working spaces at the same time as implying the company's involvement in fashion and design.

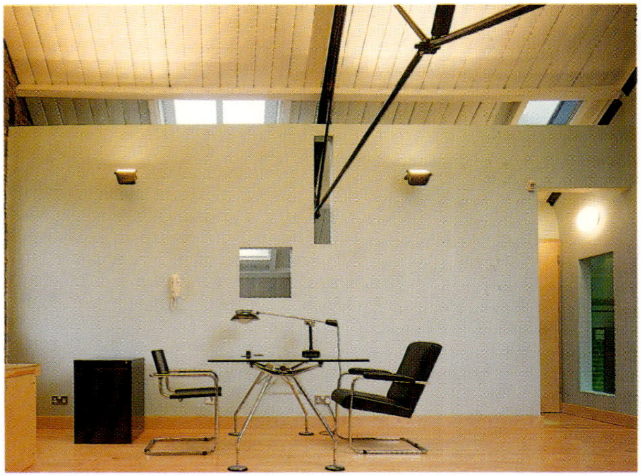

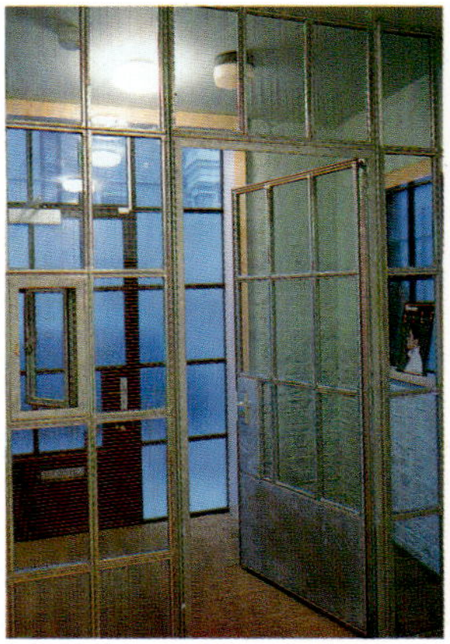

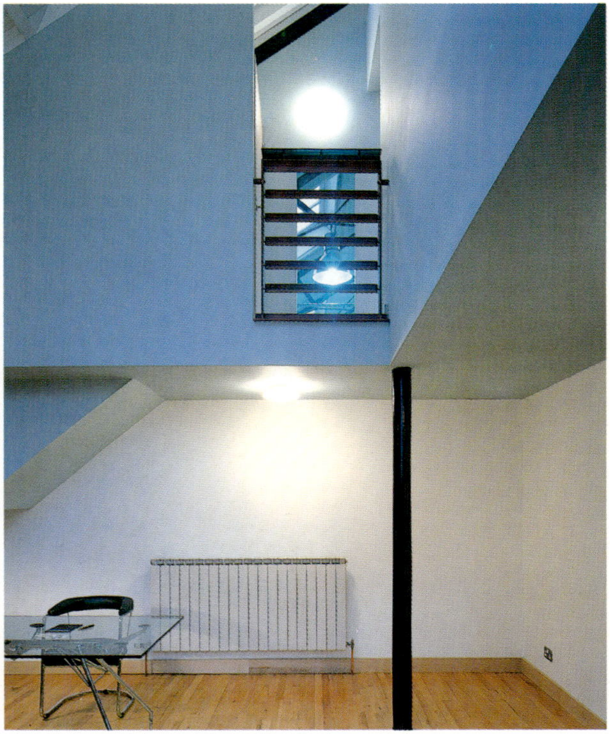

Quincy, Dean Street: a small unit in a developer's conversion with an unpleasant frontage.
Having inherited this concrete shell, we set about producing a scheme which retained the existing traditional gentlemen's outfitters feeling of the Quincy shops with a new, modern interpretation. This schizophrenic brief produced the notion of a fault line which could separate the two elements.
The scheme was designed around a Derry and Thoms 1930's counter. This we sat on a base of reconstituted marble in a different grey colour to the main blue area. Behind the counter, a pear-veneered wall of cabinets rises to

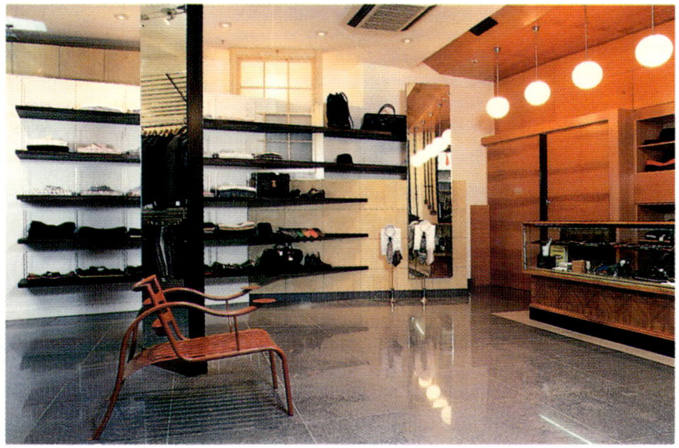

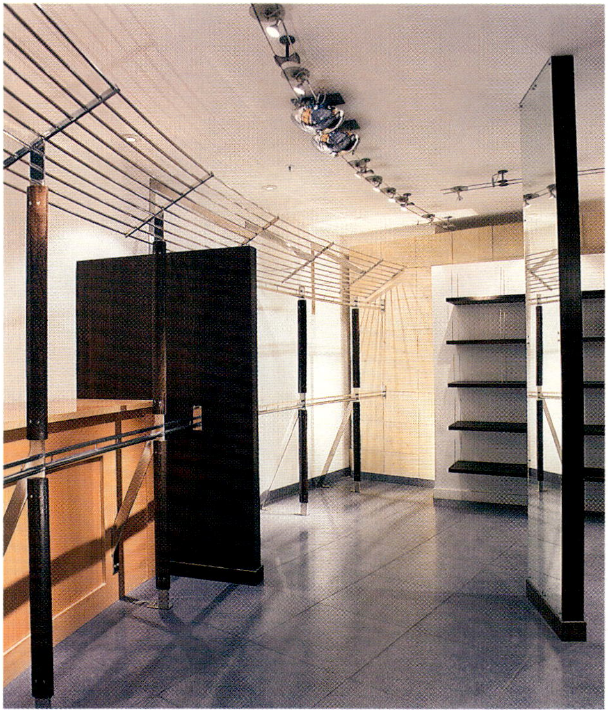

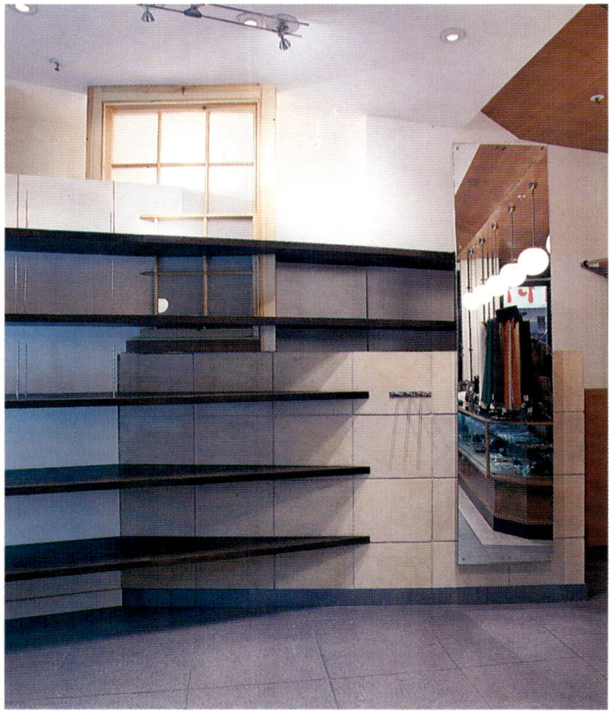

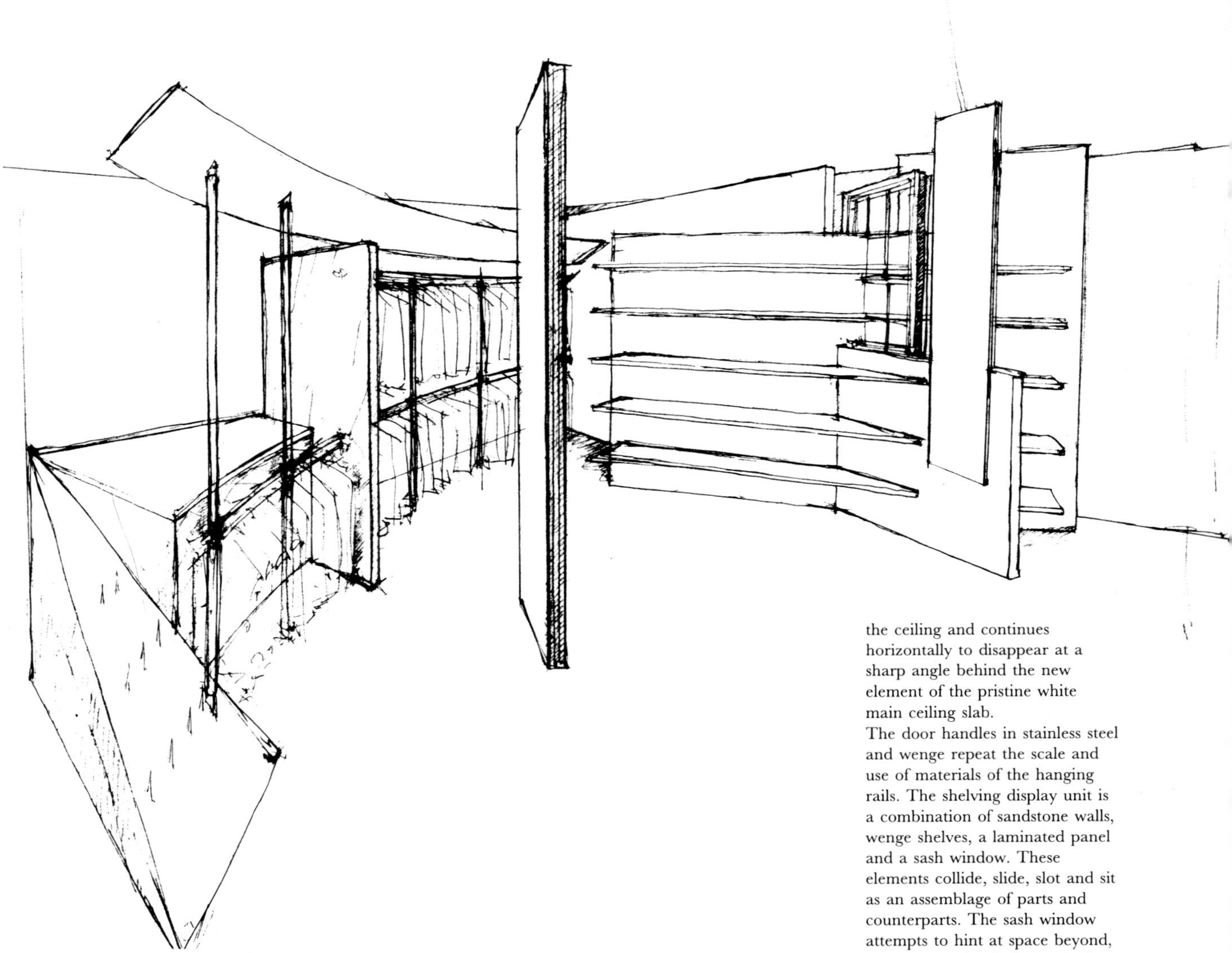

the ceiling and continues horizontally to disappear at a sharp angle behind the new element of the pristine white main ceiling slab.
The door handles in stainless steel and wenge repeat the scale and use of materials of the hanging rails. The shelving display unit is a combination of sandstone walls, wenge shelves, a laminated panel and a sash window. These elements collide, slide, slot and sit as an assemblage of parts and counterparts. The sash window attempts to hint at space beyond, not seen but implied. A naked light bulb glows unseen behind the window which bears the chocolate grinder logo reference to the days of Marcel Duchamp. Stainless steel hanging rails, cantilevered, cranked and shimmering, complete the conversation. The shop as a readymade, but not quite.

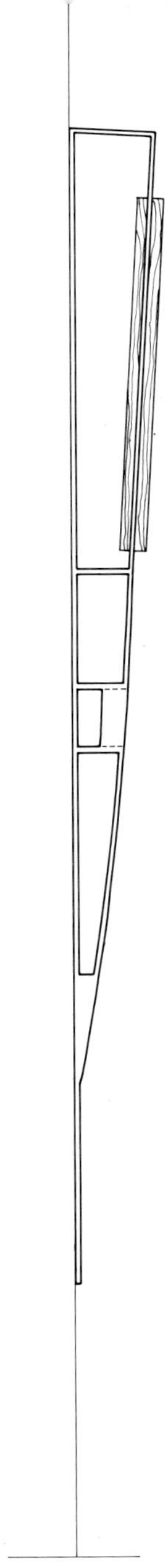

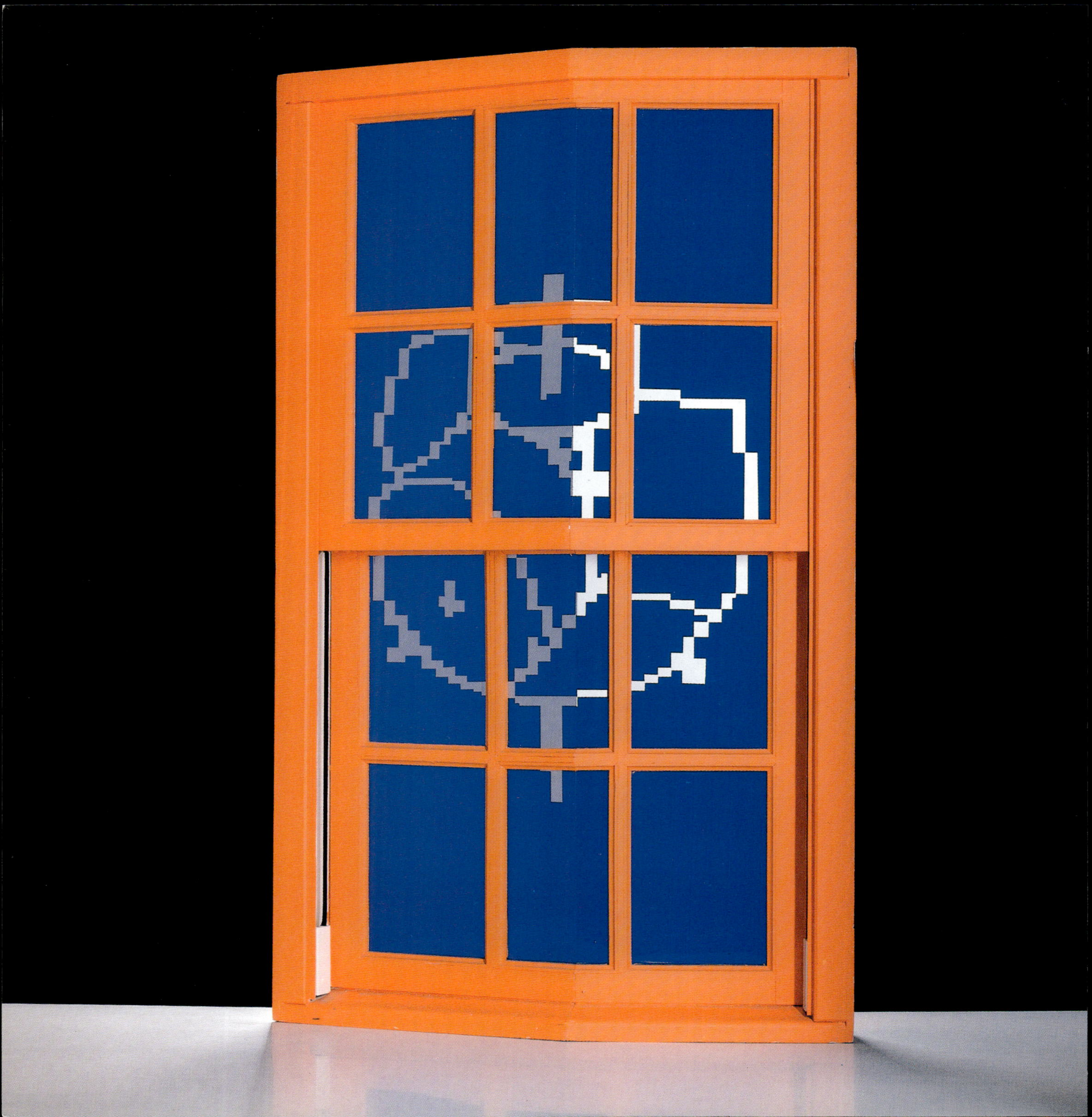

3 ALL ALONG THE DOTTED LINE

Jon Wealleans

I have been around the design scene and design education for about twenty years. Something has just dawned on me. It is simply this. It is a fantastically difficult, unprofitable and thankless task to get anything good, built or manufactured. An analogous industry would be the movies. In the period between the inception of the idea for a feature film to the point when the finished, cut and edited film is showing at your local cinema, so many forces have come into play. Bending and shaping the film to a point where it is often unrecognisable from the initial concept.

Just like architects and designers, movie directors usually succumb to the ridiculous notion of a deadline. This end date, a projection of the completion time, is usually arrived at without any regard to practical tasks being satisfactorily completed within a reasonable timescale. Usually, the deadline is established as being the time when the project has to start making money and stop costing money:

Cecil B. de Mille
was persuaded against his w
to leave out Moses
from the Wars of the Roses

It is the same story with architecture and design where batteries of individuals exist to place obstacles in the path of the designer, to the point when a good end-product can be the result of a collision of luck and accident. The process is fascinating and can convert the purest idealist into a cynic in a matter of weeks. Producing consistently good work requires almost manic stubborness, commitment and an ego like Napoleon's. Somehow at the end of the process it is very easy to succumb to the fantasy syndrome that the client is the enemy. This is a fatal philosophy which attracts few clients.

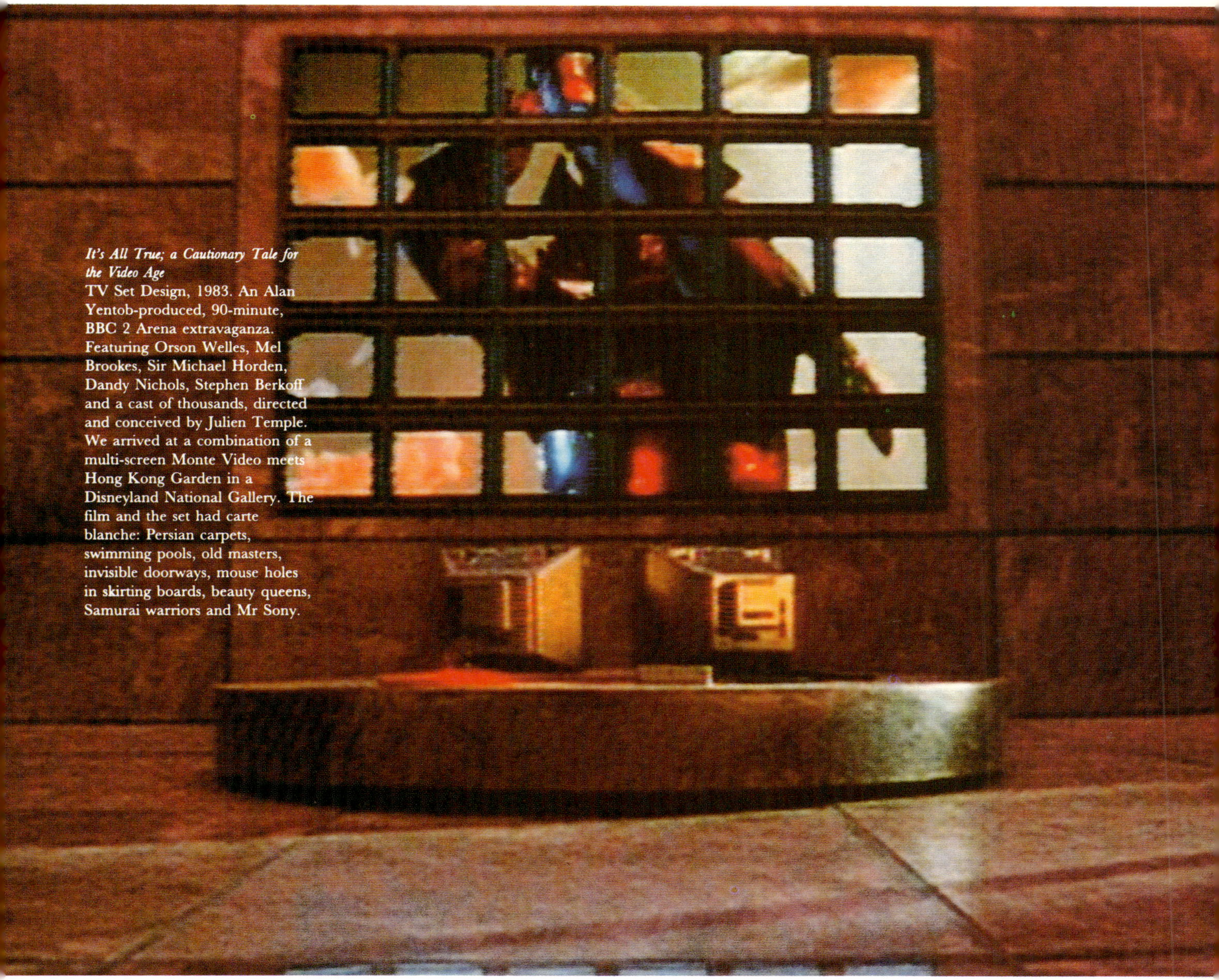

It's All True; a Cautionary Tale for the Video Age
TV Set Design, 1983. An Alan Yentob-produced, 90-minute, BBC 2 Arena extravaganza. Featuring Orson Welles, Mel Brookes, Sir Michael Horden, Dandy Nichols, Stephen Berkoff and a cast of thousands, directed and conceived by Julien Temple. We arrived at a combination of a multi-screen Monte Video meets Hong Kong Garden in a Disneyland National Gallery. The film and the set had carte blanche: Persian carpets, swimming pools, old masters, invisible doorways, mouse holes in skirting boards, beauty queens, Samurai warriors and Mr Sony.

Office
Lynne Franks P.R. office conversion, 1986. It had become necessary to rehouse the burgeoning empire of Lynne Franks P.R. in a series of cavernous semi-industrial spaces located in a mews building near Marble Arch. The contract was carried out in a tight six-week period only by using the muscle of McAlpines as the main contractor. From the reception area, a roadway of industrial lino with coloured inset markings acts as a directional device to a series of offices and meeting rooms. The road separates the offices from the blue breezeblock-enclosed open-plan workspace.

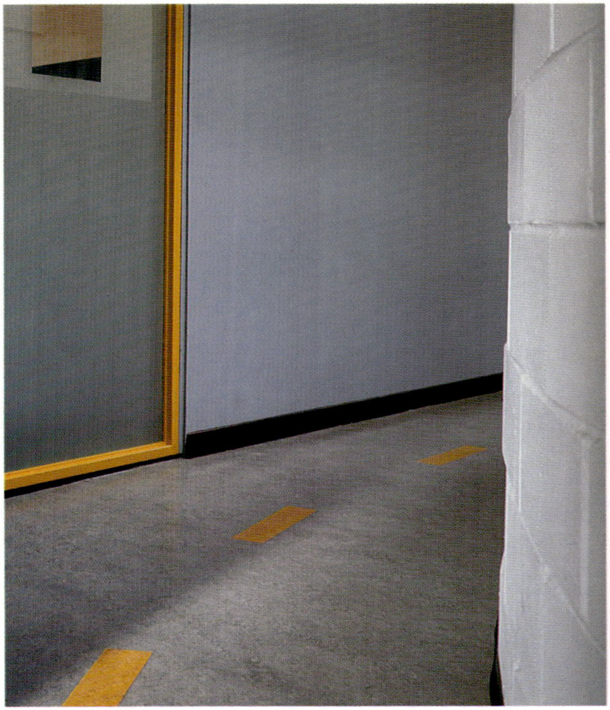

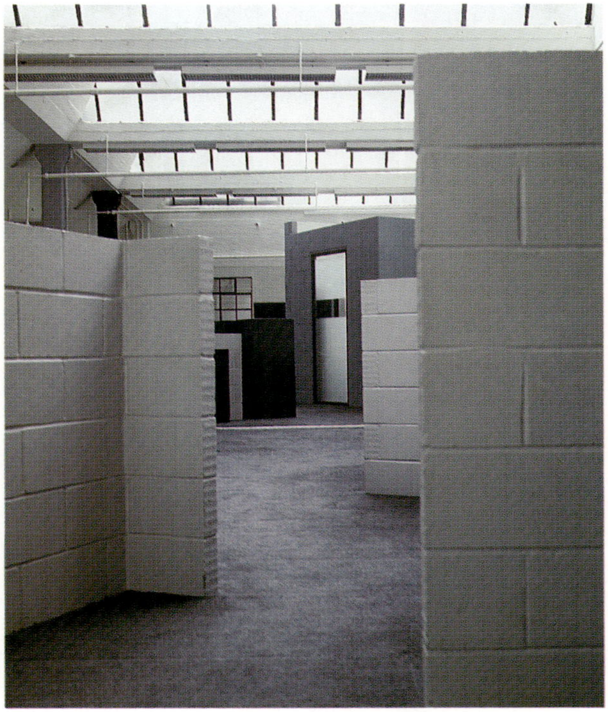

Private house
Lynne Franks and Paul Howie, 1989. A rambling house acquired by our clients needed layers of Golders Green stripping away, to allow it to breathe and become a friendly, light and colourful environment for this energetic family. New components, including a Peter Mance-designed oak, steel and glass staircase; American oak doors; green slate bathrooms; and pearlised radiators, provide a setting for an eclectic art collection and eclectic entertaining.

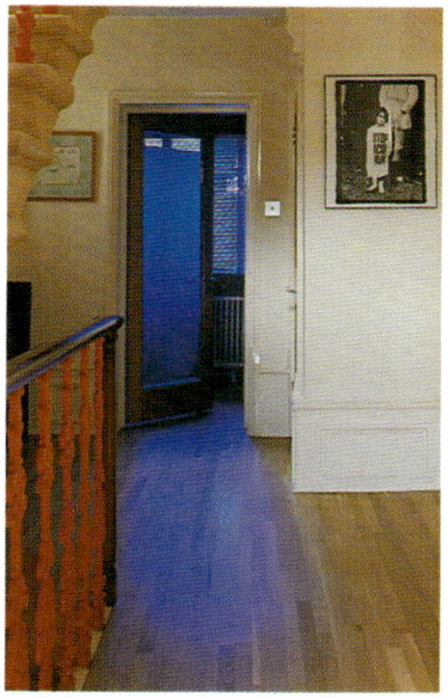

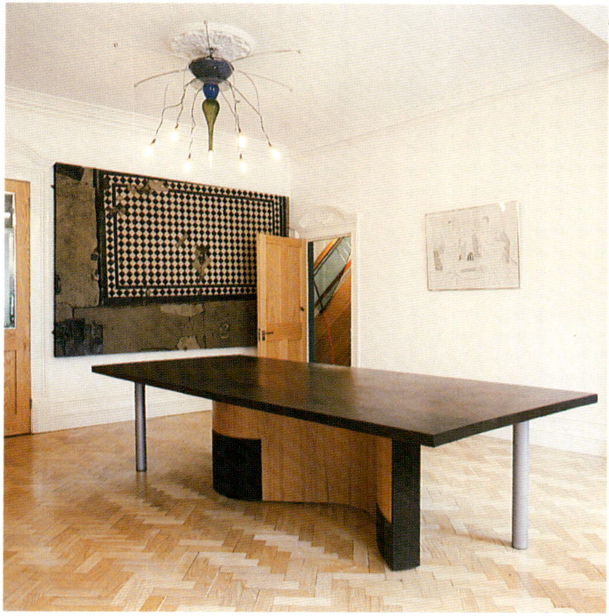

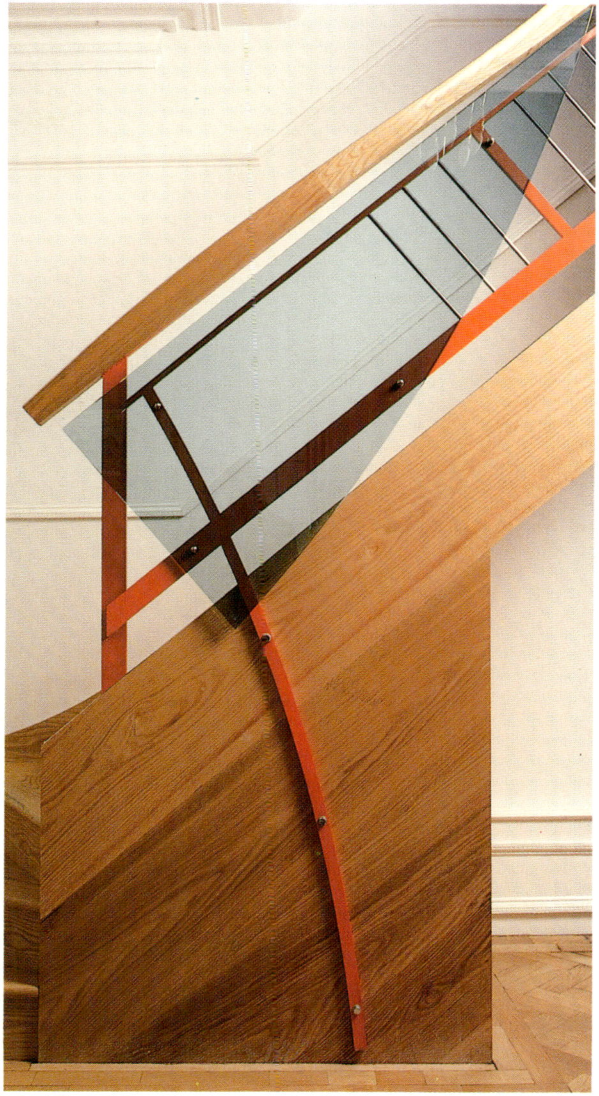

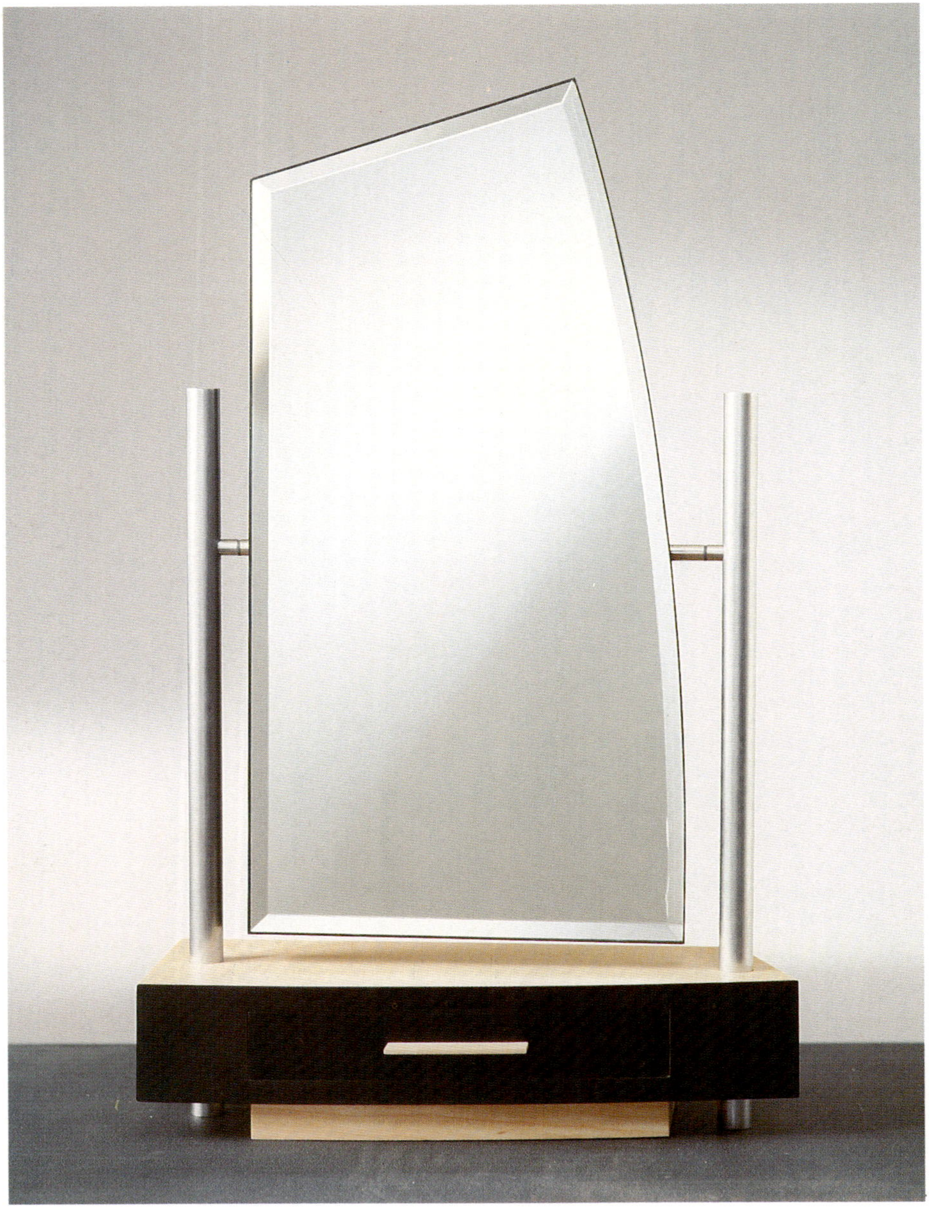

Shard Mirror
Alma furniture collection, 1987. 813 x 482 x 228mm. A mirror commissioned by the Alma Furniture Company as part of a collection of furniture designed by a group of nine architects and designers. The bevelled mirror is edged in black ColorCore and set in a sycamore frame suspended on a satin chrome-finished steel support. The base and drawer are finished in a sycamore timber, and fronted in black ColorCore.

Stool at 40 ...
Rosewood and steel, 1989.
435mm x 345mm x 355mm.
Birthday present for Ben. The three legs individually designed by Sandra Douglas, Peter Mance and Elena Massucco. The seat designed jointly.
Fabrication:
Leg 1: S.A. Issacs
Leg 2: Peter Mance, Andy Prince, Tarcal
Leg 3: S.A. Issacs
Seat: Mark 'Spindley Mouldly' Luxton (Morley Walters), Peter Mance

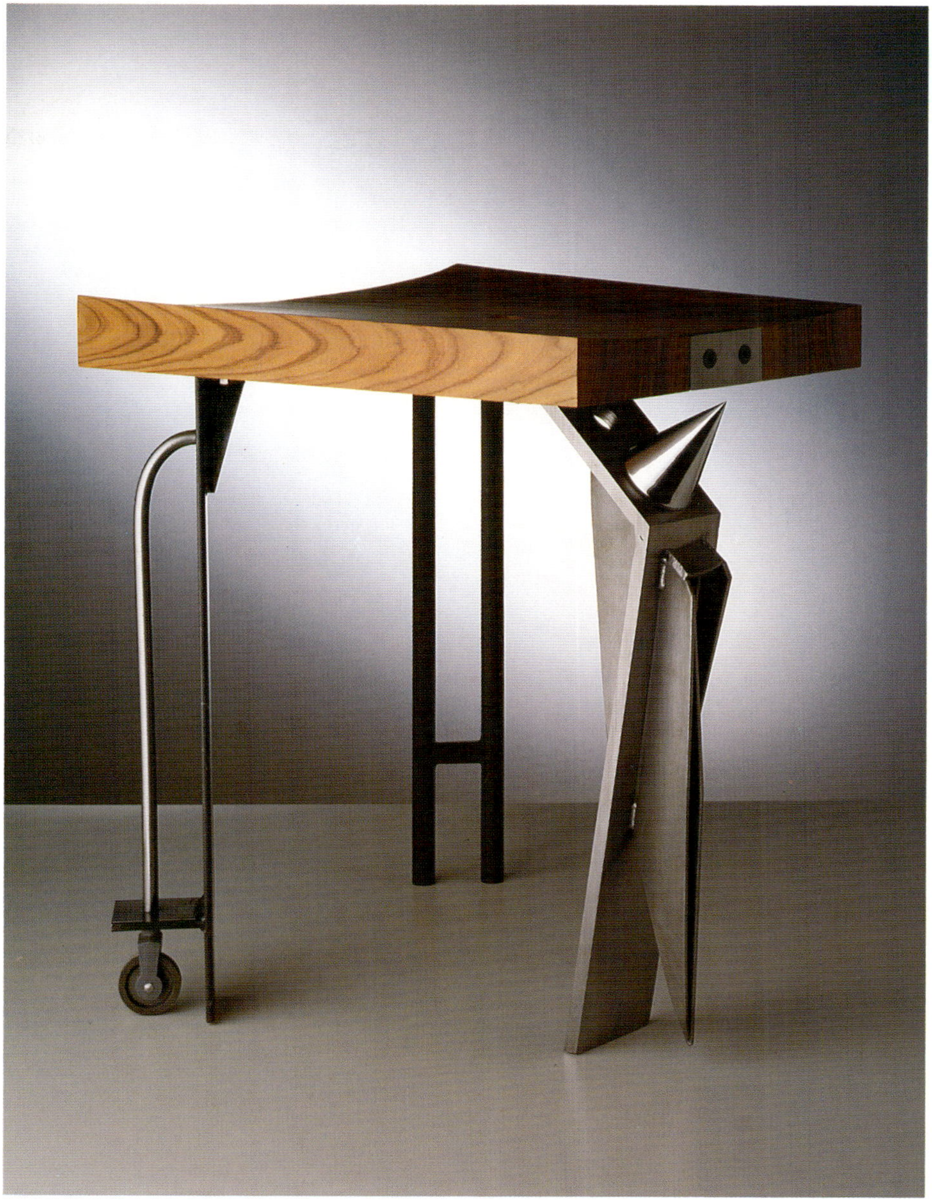

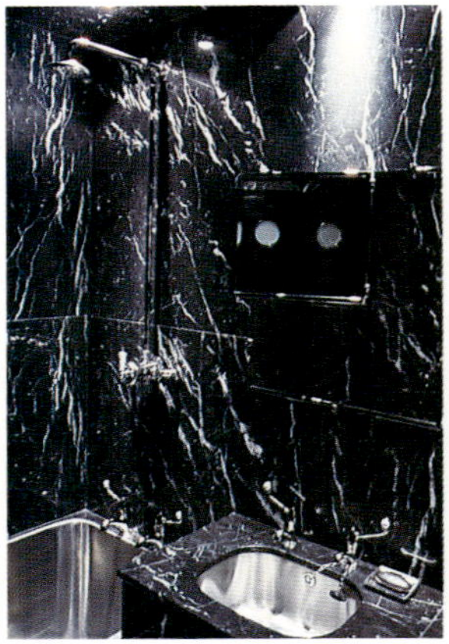

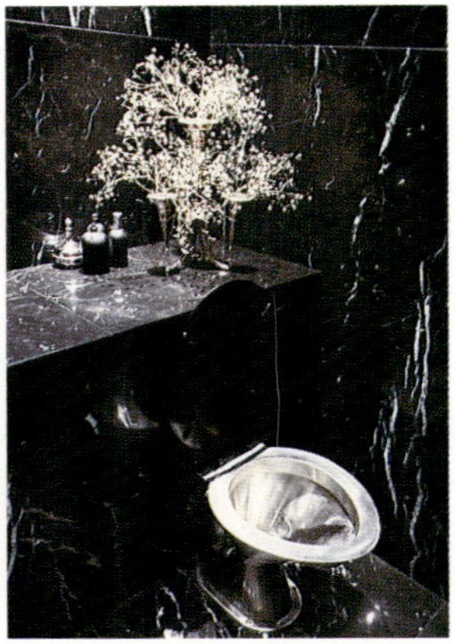

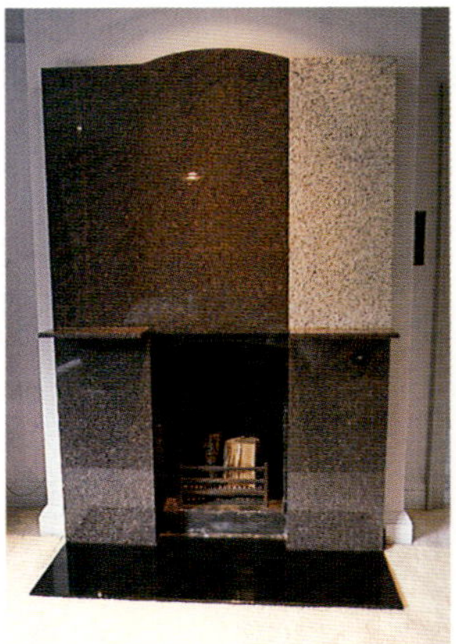

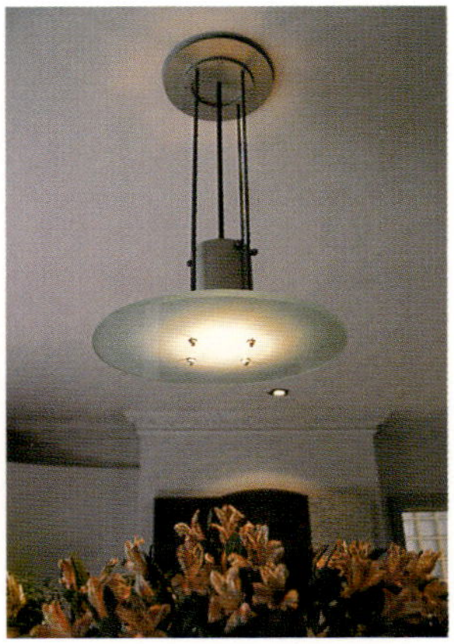

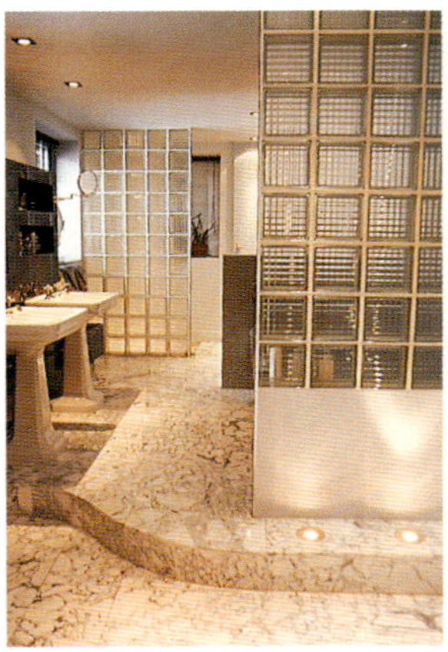

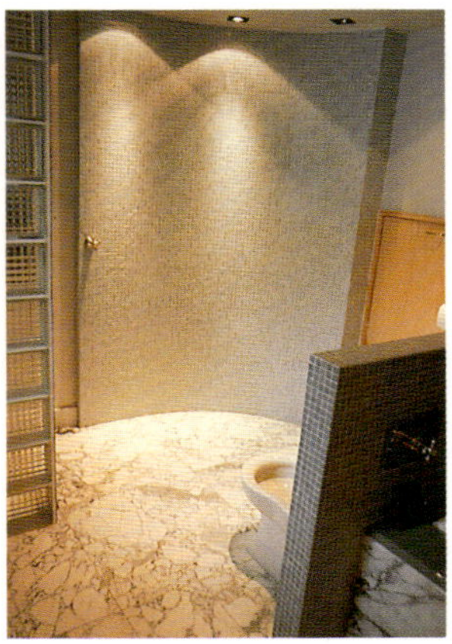

Private bathroom
Kevin and Sue Godley, 1985.

Bathroom and bedroom conversion
Lulu and John Frieda, 1985.

Two domestic conversions. The first with walls, floor and ceiling clad in black marble, with a stainless steel bath, w.c. and basin. Low voltage lighting above the shower head gave an unexpected and magical crystal shimmering effect, through the water from the shower, in this tiny guest bathroom.

In the second conversion, the clients wanted to use the bedroom as a family room, with television, video, fireplace and book shelves. Bedside switches electronically operate sliding curtains; a hidden television which magically appears at the end of the bed; and various lighting effects. The bathroom was produced using a combination of arabascata marble, glass blocks, glass mosaic and granite.

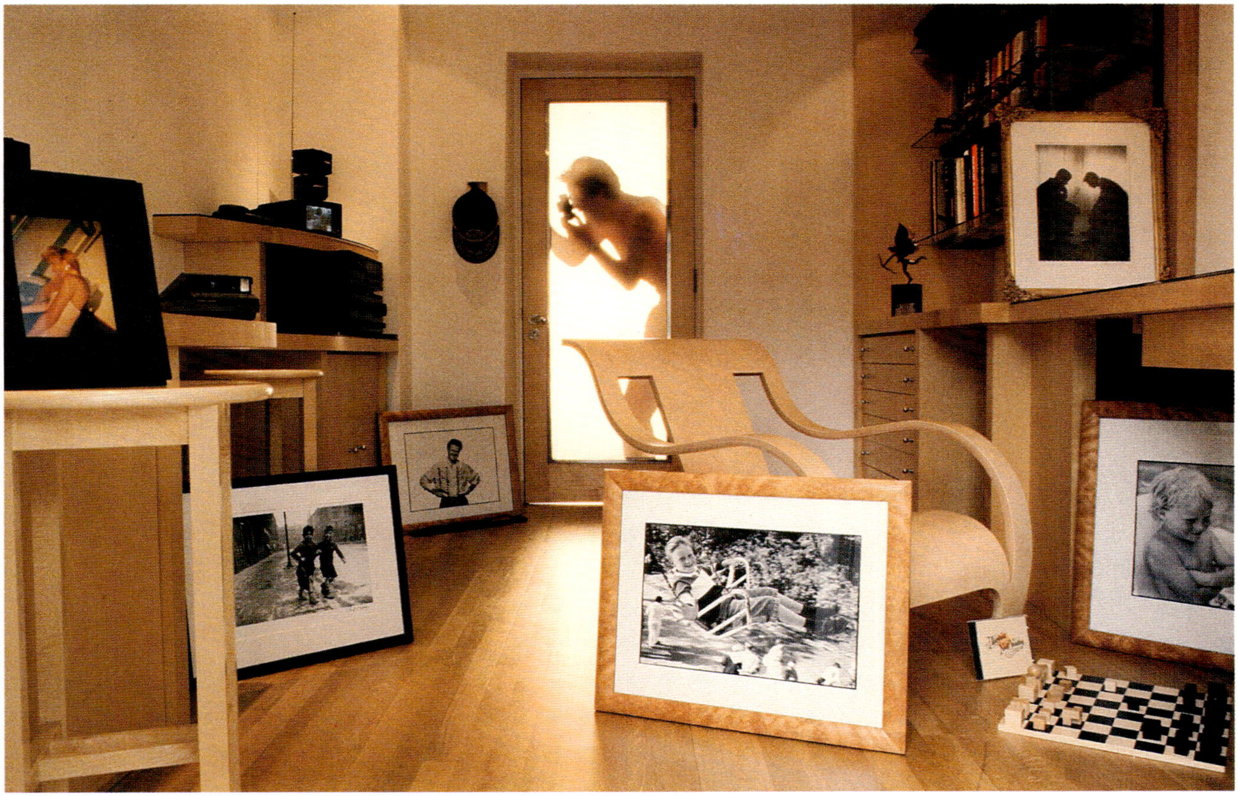

Study
Part of a private house conversion for Tony McGee 1987. This photograph of his private study was taken by Tony McGee. It reflects his creativity and is a personal observation of his own private space. This approach is also revealed in the text of his affectionate rap.

Ben out of Ten
In my best ten, there's a place for Ben. A man so passionate , never out to find cash in it. Tears for beers often finds the way, but he'll be the first on site, the very next day. Mad about bendy things, shiny things too. Crazy for his friends, especially Johnny Prew. Give him a job (not that he needs one): he won't let you down. I know just the one: it's that new, New Town. An architect is what McDonald's needs, not a clown. Ah...but I know Ben!

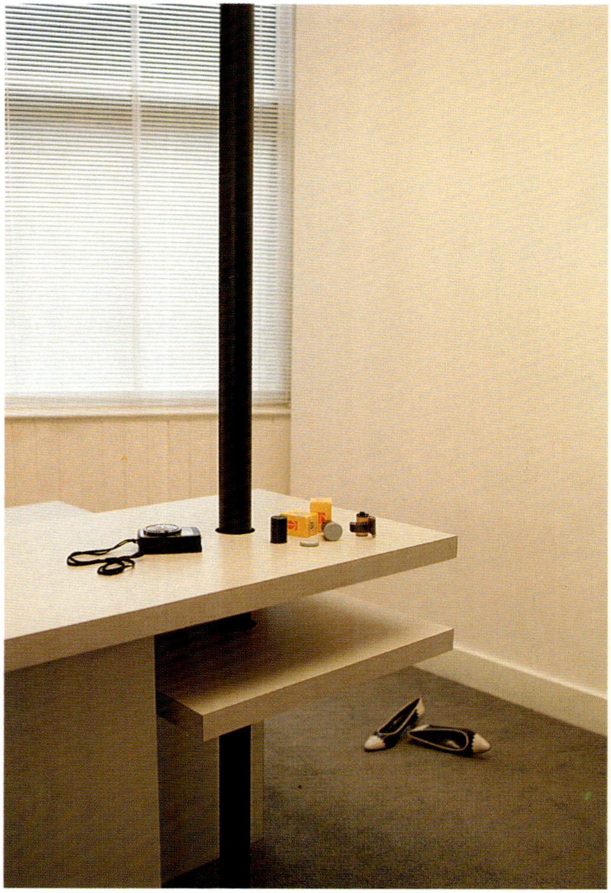
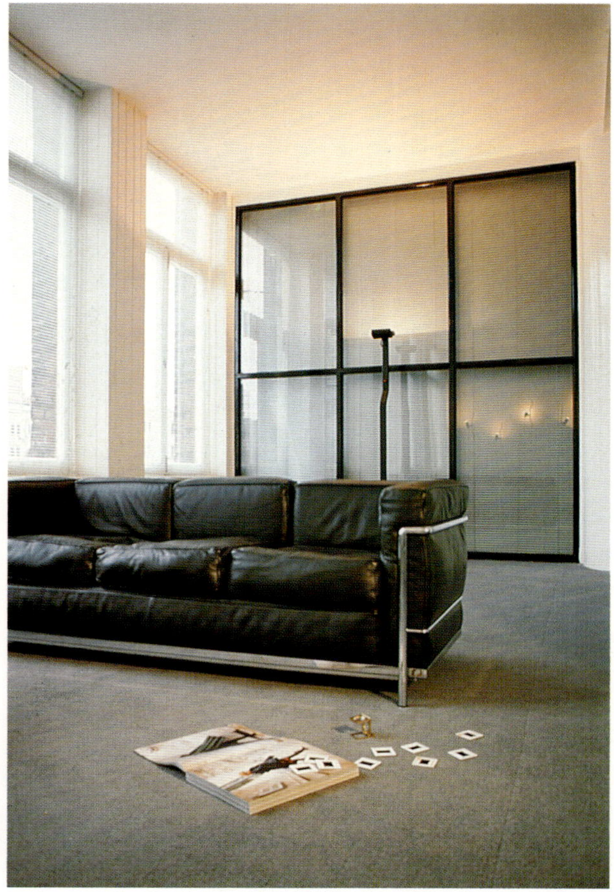

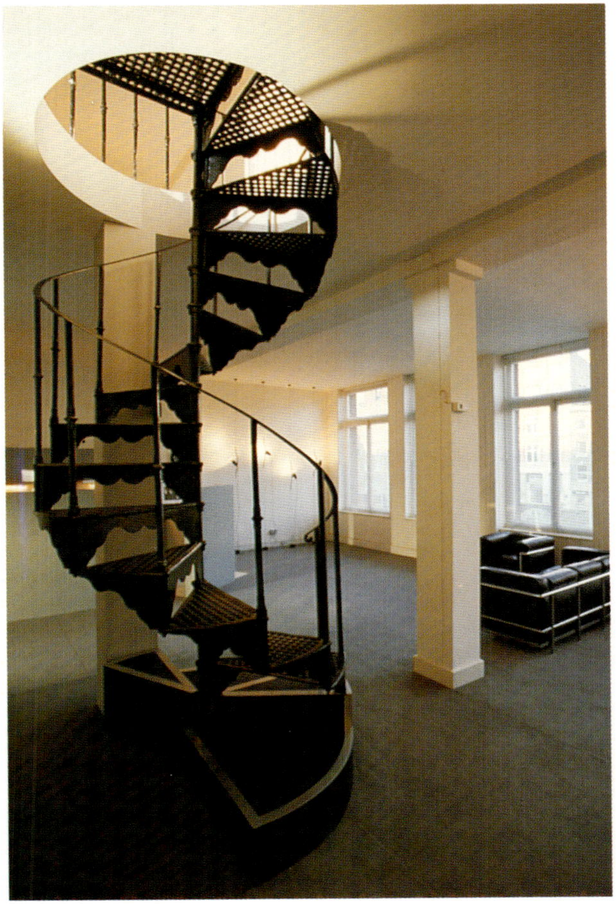

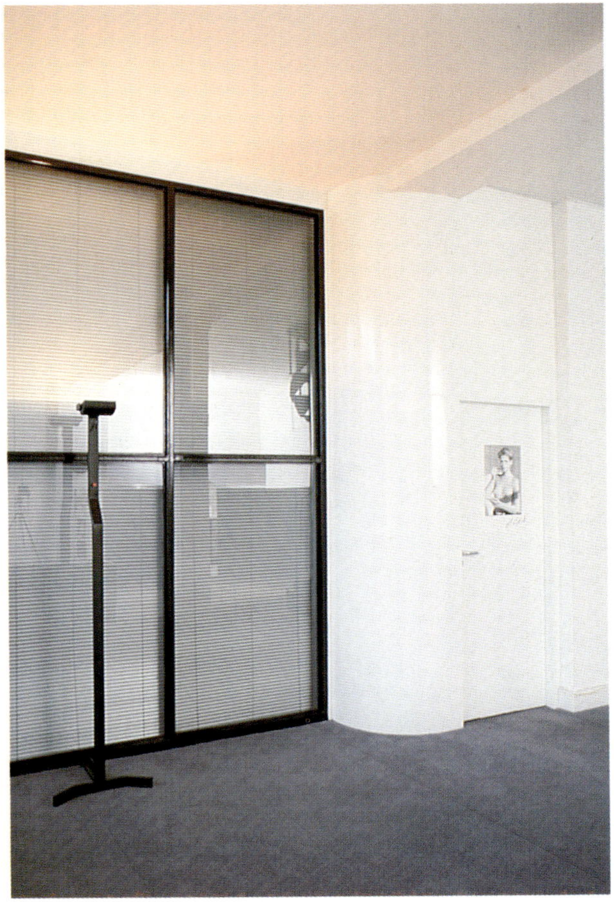

Photographic Studio
Tony McGee, 1982. Two floors are connected by a centrally located spiral staircase. The top floor contains the main studio space, with the lower floor combining reception, models' changing area, kitchen, waiting and meeting area and office space. The space was chosen specifically for its daylight qualities, allowing the client the freedom to work with both natural and artificial light. A simple combination of angled walls, curved partitions and glazed steel frames provide a background for the activities which range from a serene, calm atmosphere, to the manic activity of a photographic session.

Kevin Godley

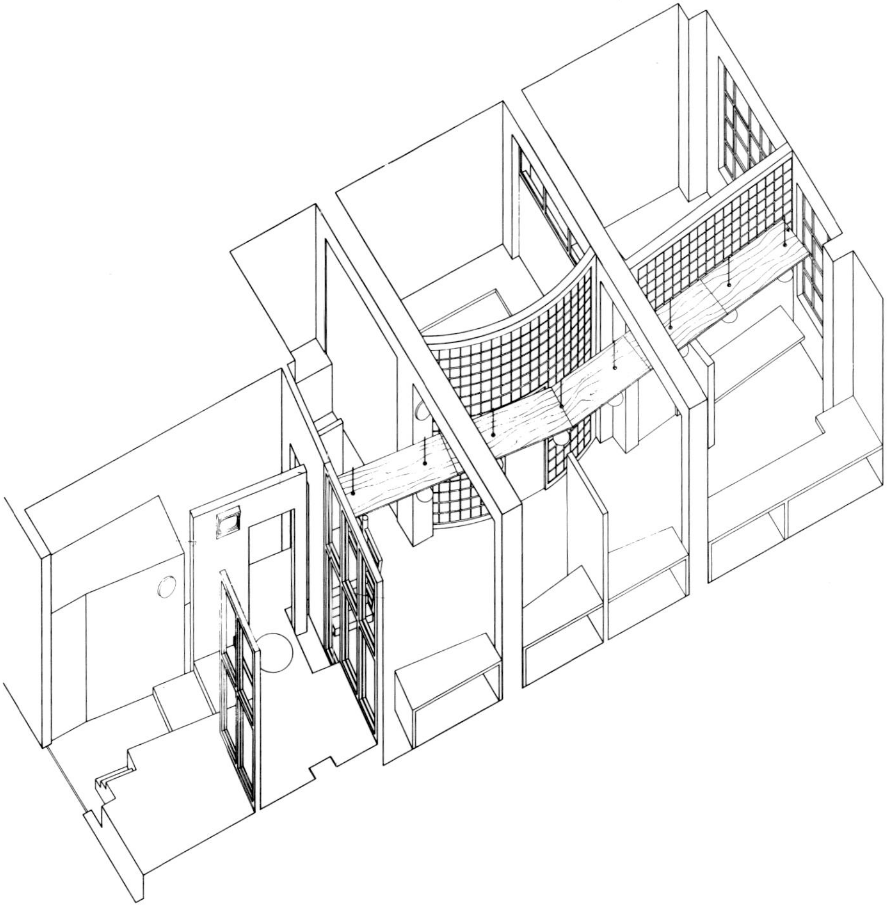

Ben is an artist who creates spaces for people. This is something more than a designer. It implies a style, a flair and an attitude that is unique. An environment that has a signature. Ben does what I do with pictures and music, but you can't switch what he does off. You have to live or work in it so it had better be right. His masterpiece, The Haçienda, is a sculpture that brilliantly includes its clientele as part of the design. He retains his vision whilst dealing with the tastes and budgets of so many different people. Houses, shops, clubs, bars etc. Ben is an interior designer with many hits to his name, although the last time we met he was moaning about the rate at which his business was expanding...
There's no pleasing some people.

Medialab
Office and Studio conversion for video production company, 1985. Kevin Godley and his former partner Lol Creme wanted a series of spaces which would communicate the company's activities and identity, and provide practical work areas for production and design. The reception and waiting area sit on a raised floor and are separated from the main workspace by a steel-framed, etched-glass screen. The route from reception to the offices is through an opening in a slab wall containing a TV monitor. The design office is behind a curved glass-block wall, with Kevin and Lol's think-tank behind a similar straight glass block wall. Two Charles Eames' lounge chairs with ottomans provide the seating accommodation for our two directors to sit and create tomorrow's promos.

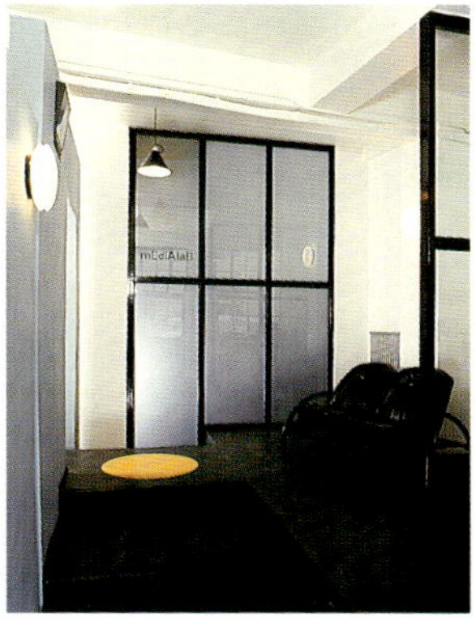

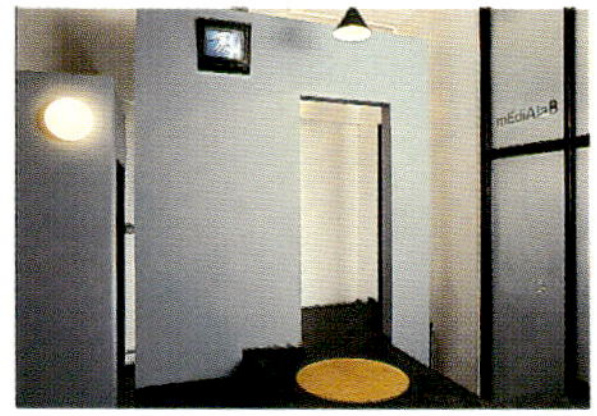

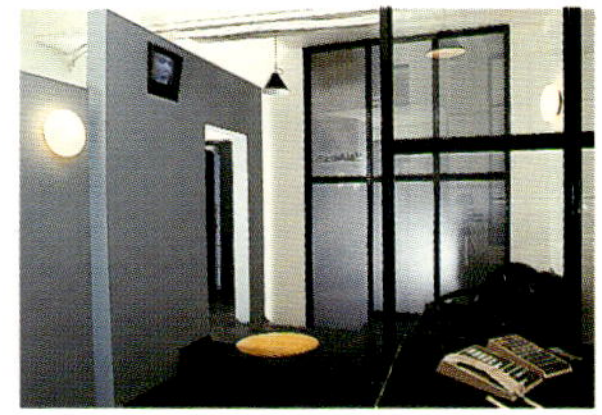

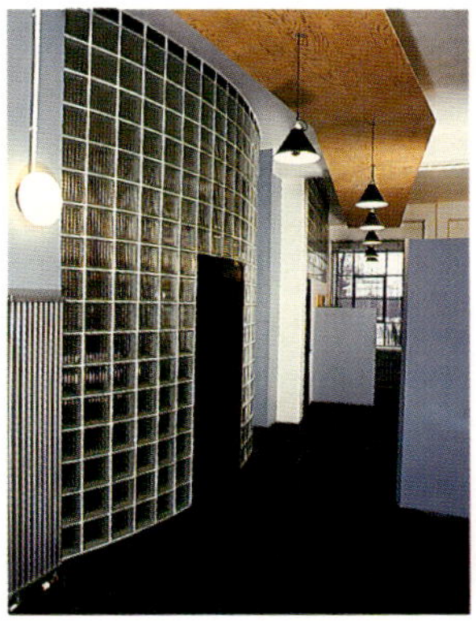

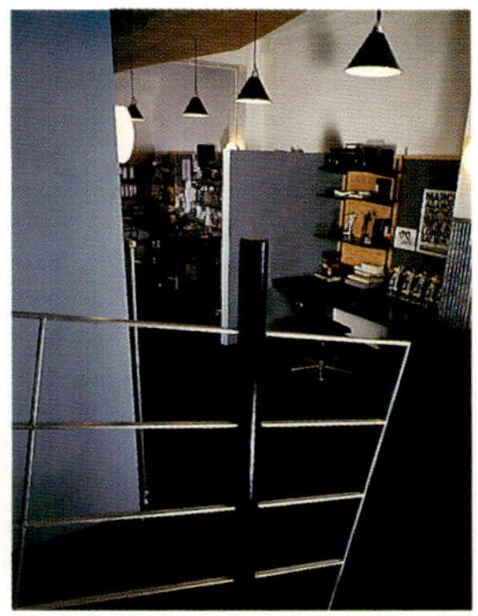

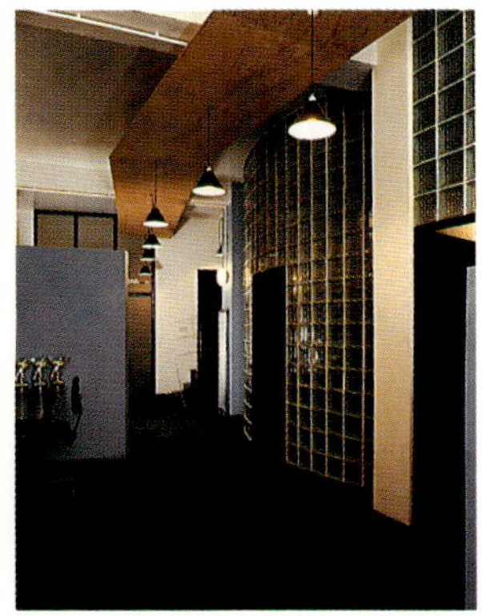

Peter Saville

'I used to just take things from Ben, like he was a reference book or something. He used to get really mad about it...'

'With the right inspiration, record covers are easy. The big 'problem' is guiding them through a system that wants innovation but hates inconvenience. With IsmIsm he pushed his luck a little too far.'

'He's better with the bigger pieces that you can walk around in – the art installations that he calls interior design. The Haçienda was so groovy that instead of being a monument to the 80's, it was the birthplace of the 90's.'

'This book is the catalogue that Ben's studio can't afford to produce. He should take it to America or France or Italy or Japan. He shouldn't come back here until Tony Wilson is Prime Minister.'

'Where is the Ben Kelly furniture, the movie sets and the art? Britain is just not the place for those things – only shopkeeping and pop music. There should be a big business around him by now, like Starck. Someone should make him global or make him move.'

Ben Kelly

Turning Steel into Cardboard

From The Associated Perforators and Weavers select a perforation. Coat the steel with its required finish and bake in a hot oven. For the purpose of this exercise fit the fired panels onto the prefabricated glazed timber door of the clothes shop. Allow the assemblage to rest in place for as long as possible. This has now become a 'High Tech' installation.

Dialogue between hungry graphic designer and hungry interior designer: one proposes an idea of constructing a record sleeve out of the minimal amount of cardboard possible. He is sent to see the perforated steel panels in the door of the clothes shop. The interior designer replies that the only way forward is to perforate the sleeve. Apply the same process to cardboard as to steel. The graphic designer sets to. He draws up his perforated grid, dies are cast, cardboard is perforated. Use only blue and orange. Any other colours are totally unacceptable. The steel has now become cardboard. Record sales soar. Award ceremonies are attended. Yellow pencils are handed out. Silver music notes shower down. This is the industrial ethic.

If you have been given the image of a stylised head, wearing a long pointed hat taken from an Italian Fascist poster circa 1929, you have to know what to do with it. Especially if it is to become an image on a record sleeve. You cannot reprint it as a flat two-dimensional image. This is particularly the case if you are trained as an interior designer and not well-versed in the typographic arts. My approach has been to use objects, real materials and processes. Do not open the Pantone book.

The Fascist connection took me to the Imperial War Museum. Images in relief on rows of soldier's medals. Plaster moulded scenes of soldiers fighting. Images of war that pointed the way forward.

Have the man with the pointed hat moulded in wax, make a plaster mould, cast the head. A three-dimensional head with a pointed hat appears. Take a piece of slate, employ a stone letter carver to fashion out the letters. Carefully break the slate allowing a contrast of hard edges. This gives tension. Set the assemblage on a background of galvanised steel and shoot it quick.

From plaster, slate, oil, gold leaf, anodised aluminium, galvanised steel and craftsmen, via the imperial War Museum, comes the folded cardboard sleeve. The sleeve depicts a photographic image. The interpretation of an Italian Fascist poster in 1929 fast forward to 1982. V deep, the Boomtown Rats and oblivion.

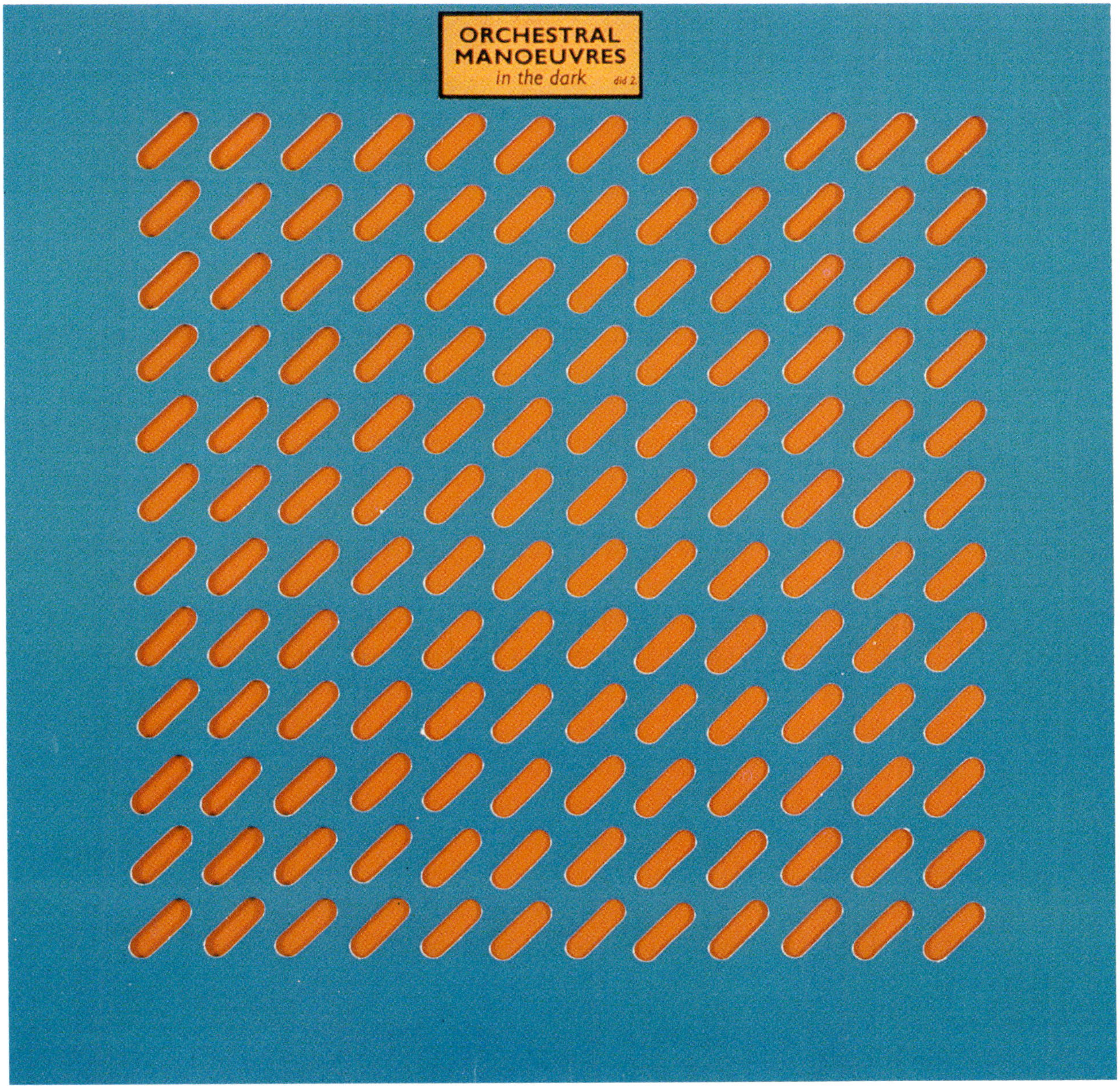
ORCHESTRAL
MANOEUVRES
in the dark
did 2.

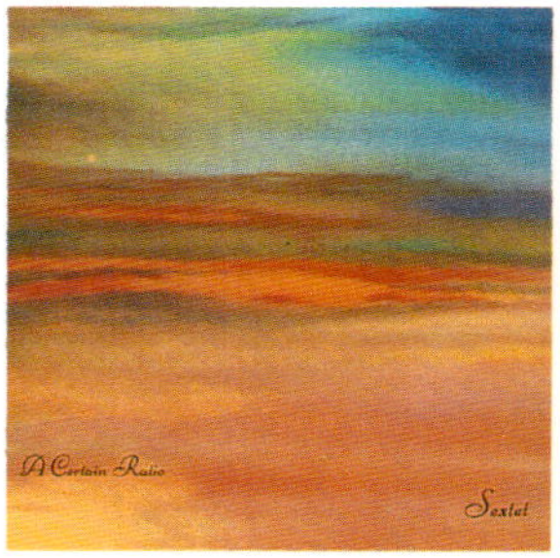

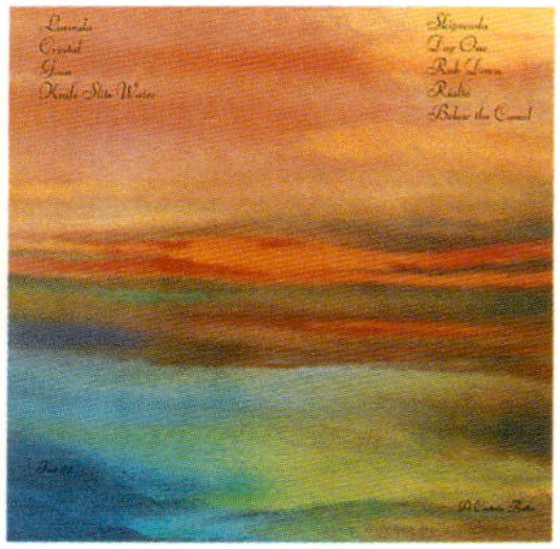
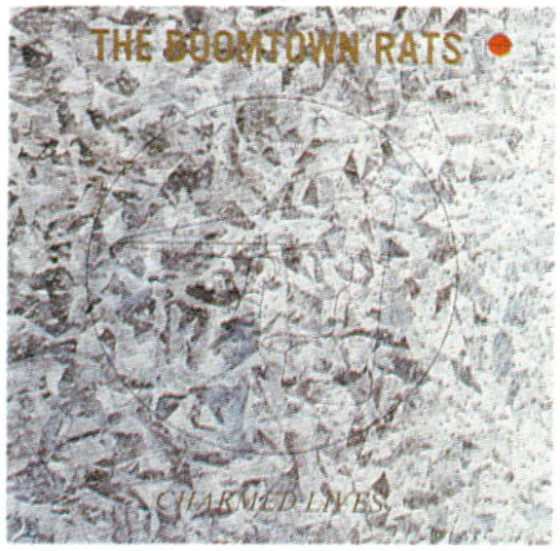

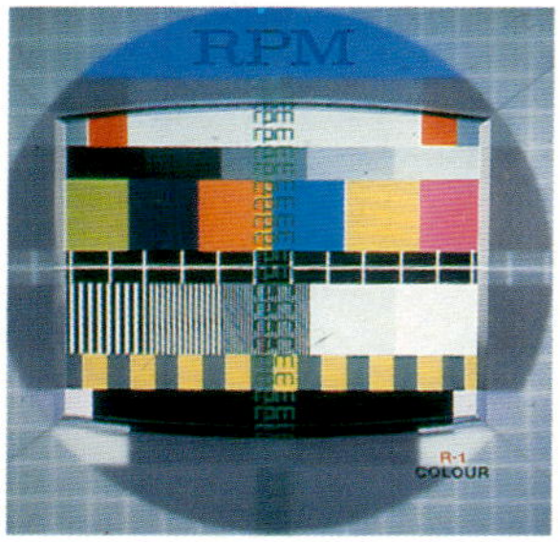

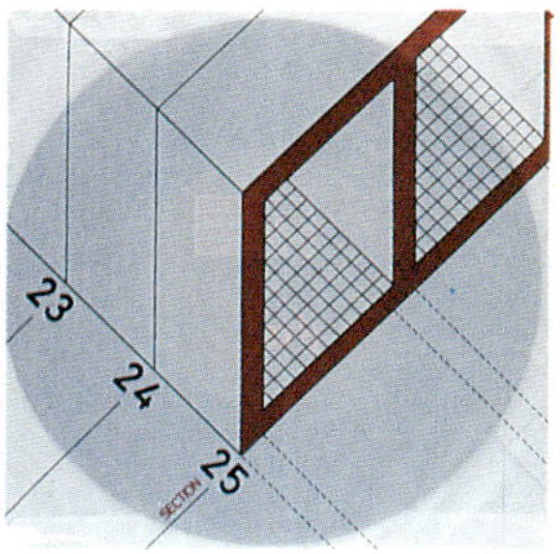

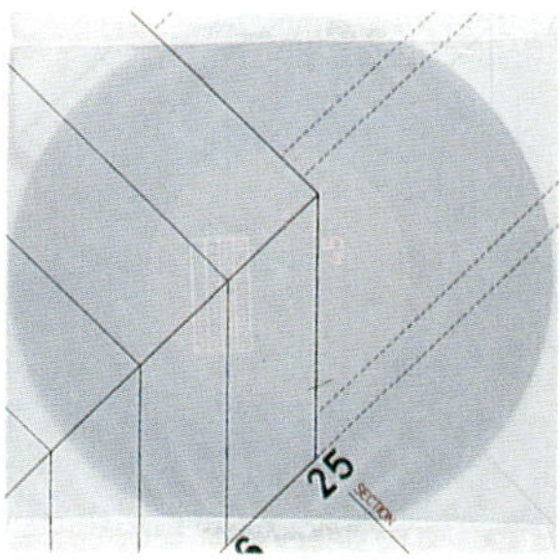

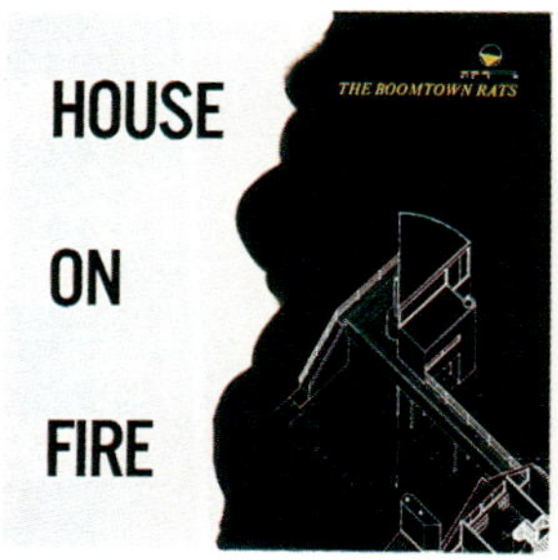

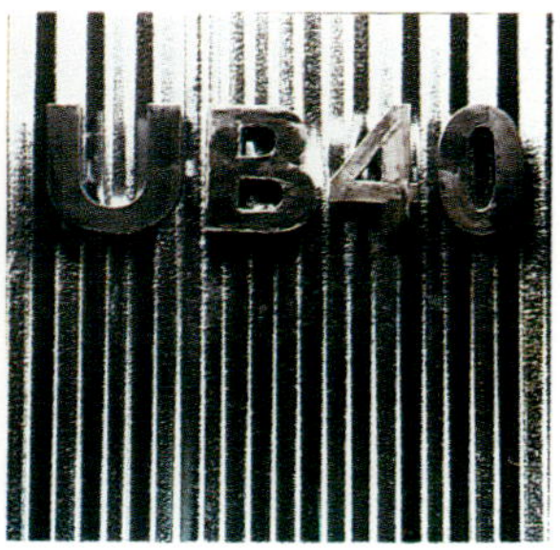

Record sleeves
Having become a record sleeve designer by default, it felt logical to continue with the same process. For an interior designer it was a joy to work with the scale of a 300mm square, and felt like serious therapy.
During this period I attempted a similar approach to record sleeves as to interior design. Peter Saville and Brett Wickens supplied technical and aesthetic support through a different minefield to the one I am normally used to.

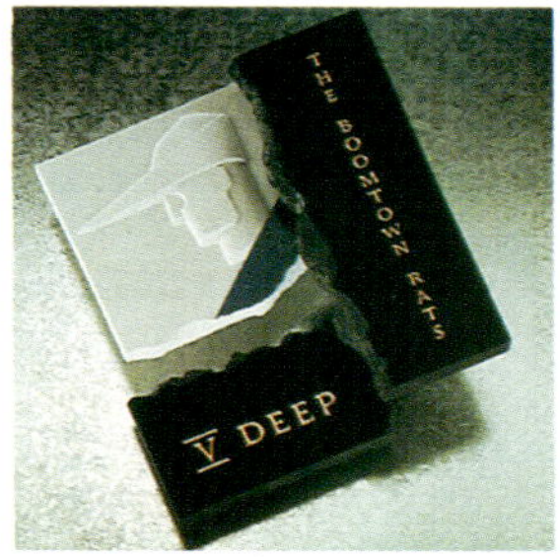

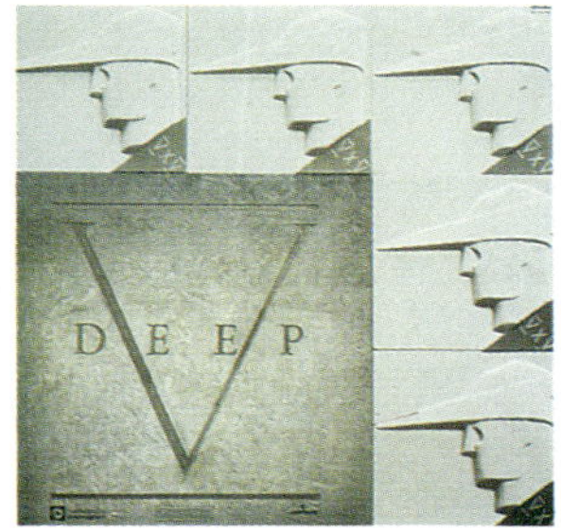

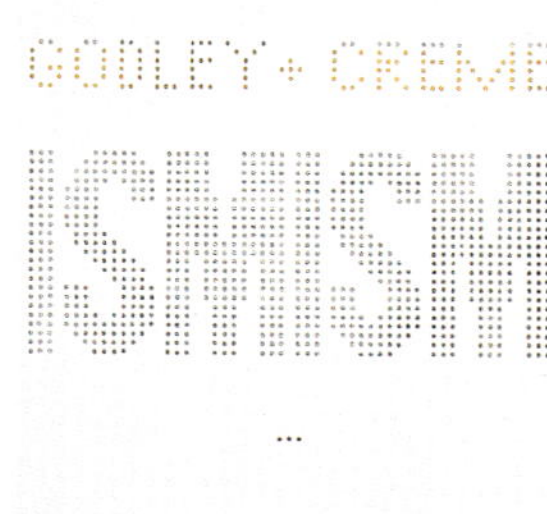

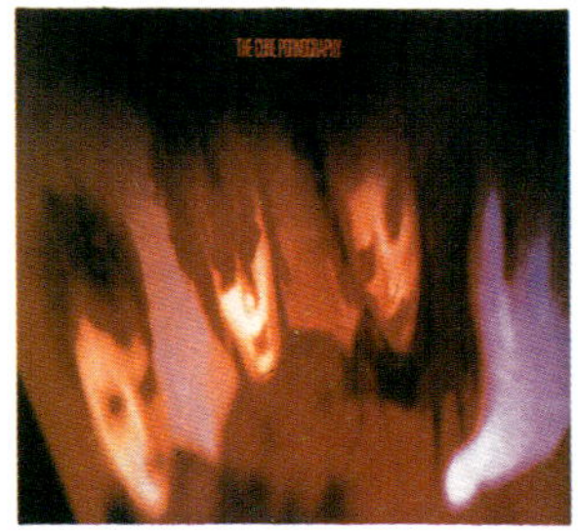

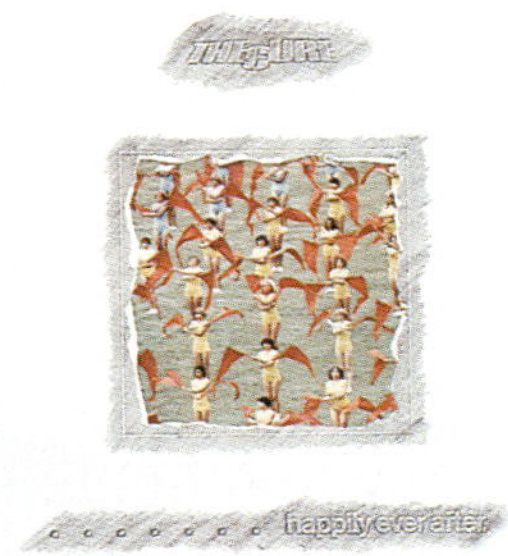

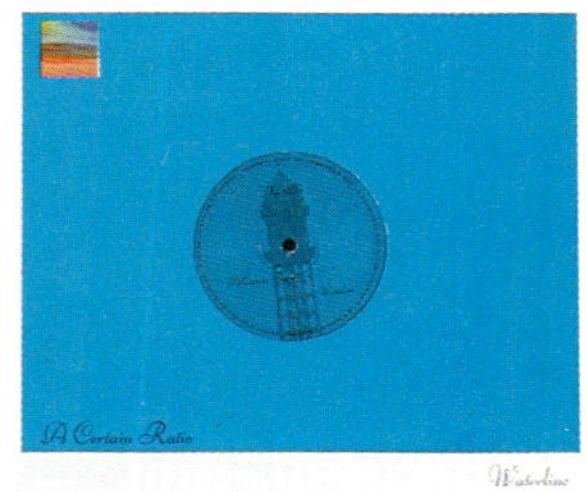

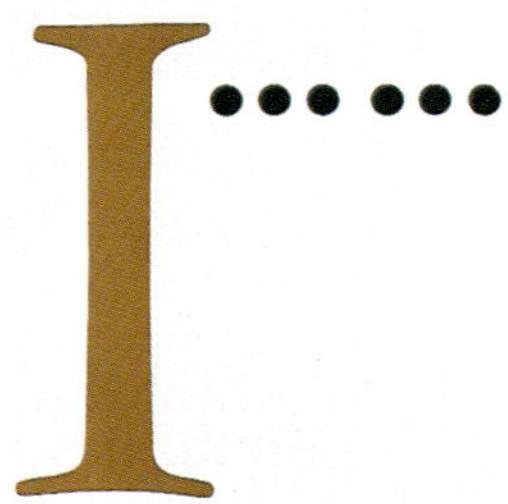

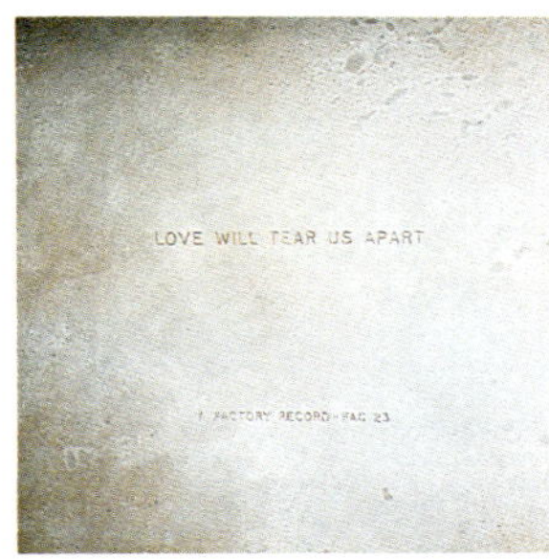

A Certain Ratio *Sextet*
The Boomtown Rats
Charmed Lives
RPM *In Colour*
Section 25 *Girls don't count*
The Boomtown Rats
House on Fire
UB40 *UB40 1980-83*
The Boomtown Rats *$\overline{V}$ Deep*
Godley and Creme *Ism Ism*
The Cure *Pornography*
The Cure *...happily ever after*
A Certain Ratio *Waterline*
The Boomtown Rats
Never in a Million Years
Joy Division
Love will tear us apart

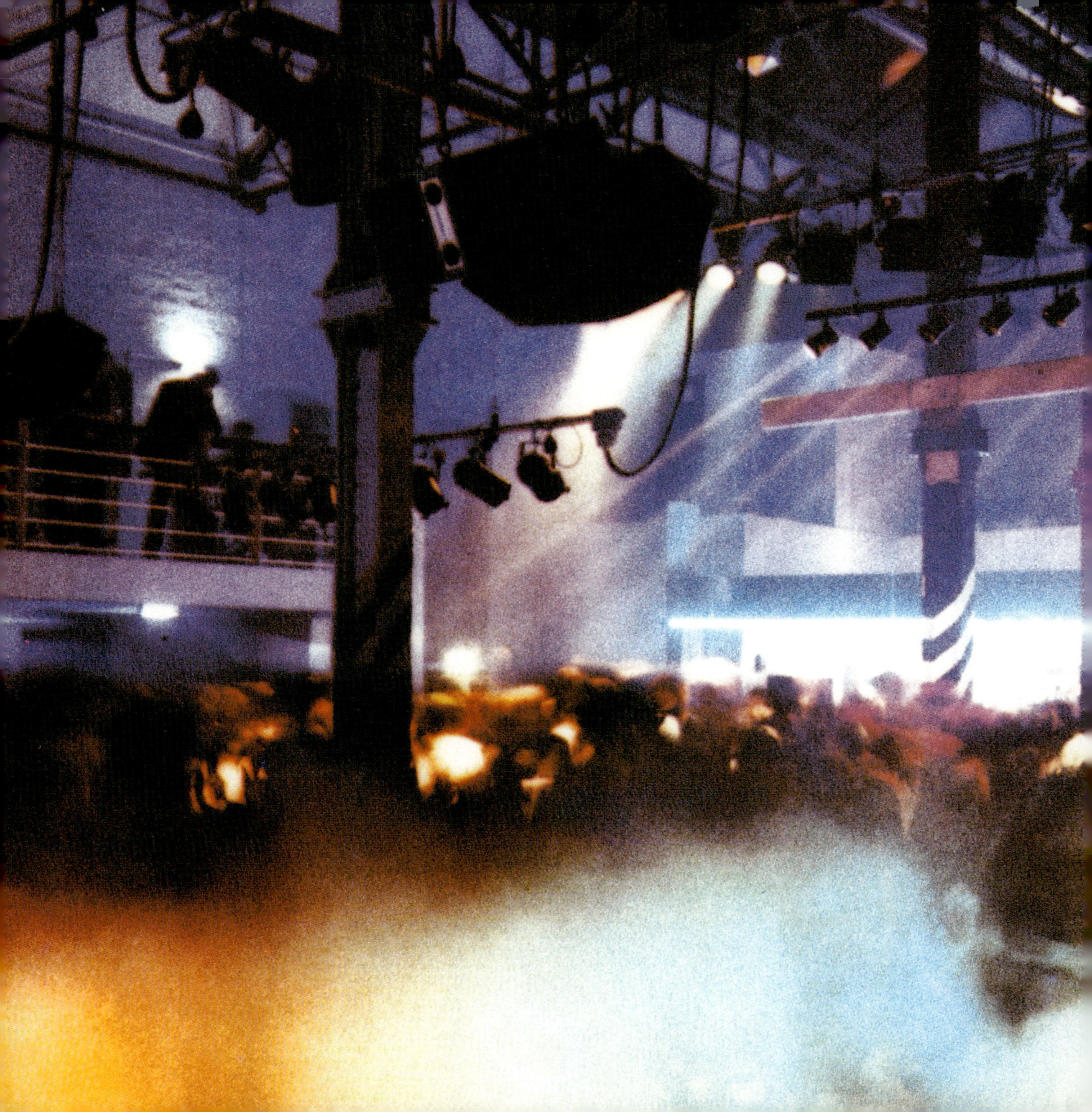

And you forgotten, your memories ravaged by all the chaos of the planet, wrecked in the Red Caves of Pali-Kao, without any knowledge of either music or geography, no longer leaving for the haçienda *where the roots dream of the child and where the wine ends in tales from some old almanac.* Well, you've blown it now. You'll never see the hacienda. It doesn't exist anywhere...

4 THE HAÇIENDA MUST BE BUILT

Ben Kelly

The Haçienda must be built

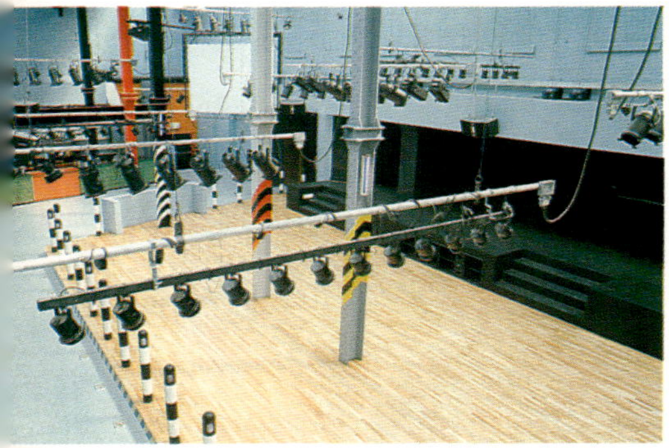

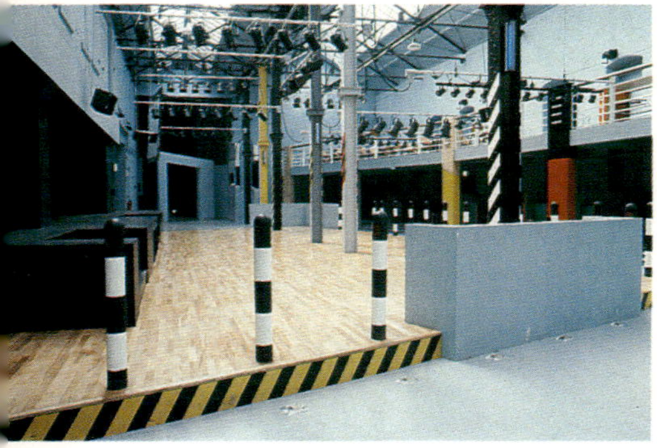

Q: How many people can you get in a yachting showroom?
A: As many as the fire officer will allow, 1500 bodies. It appears necessary to turn a yachting showroom into what will become the hottest, hippest brainchild of the crew of Starship Factory Communications. Arguments ensue. Is it a disco? Is it a club? Is it a bar? Is it a venue? Who cares. Let's make it everything. Provide a setting, make it flexible, let the people decide. A night out in Manchester for the Factory followers. Through the galvanized roller shutter, through the Fac51 doors, through the slab enclosure, through the monolithic archway, past the dance floor, past the stage, to the Kim Philby bar.

A journey through an industrial landscape boosted by theatre and technology. Visual puns to break your journey. A line of steel columns colour coded to warn you; take care; you never know who you might bump into on the disco floor; The Gay Traitor or Kim Philby himself. Cats' eyes to stare at you with bollards to protect you. Monolithic slab supports to the balcony, marching in line, speak a narrative of perforations. An angled arch with attendant monoliths to greet your ceremony, to be met by another in a state of decay. All wrapped in a coat of Pigeon Blue BS409.

We are leaving the twentieth century

Sandra Douglas

The design was essentially a direct response to the building. It was never our intention to lose the scale or proportions offered but to enhance and capitalise on it. It was important to offer some sort of flexibility to our client and the user. A formal 'Disco' environment was out of the question. We introduced fly bars with theatrical lights to enable the management through lighting technicians to create different moods and atmospheres, which they dictate rather than be dictated by. The dancefloor is as prominent as the stage so there is as much emphasis on music as perfomance. There was constant movement within the interiors as people travelled from balcony level to restaurant and from one bar to the other. The most memorable moment throughout construction was when the sound system was finally switched on and the whole point became obvious; no pretension, no fuss, no glamour – just as intended.

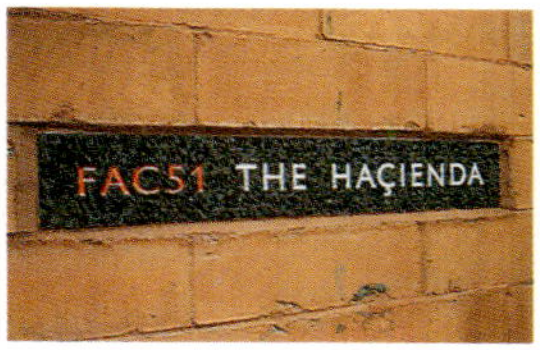
FAC51 THE HAÇIENDA
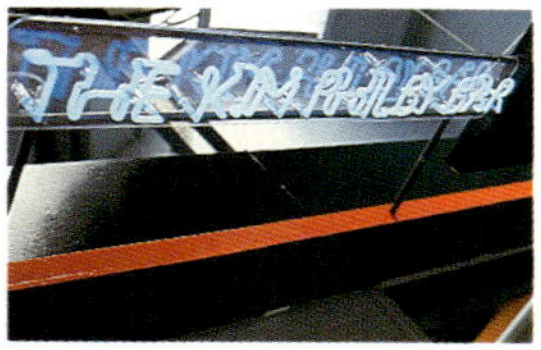
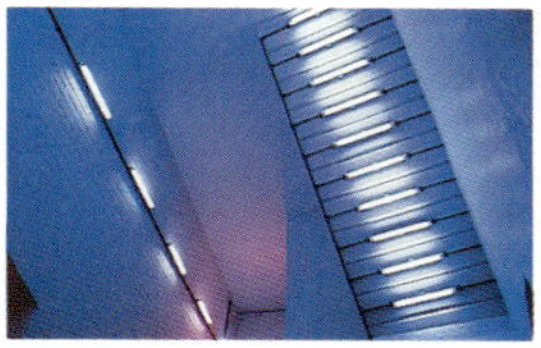
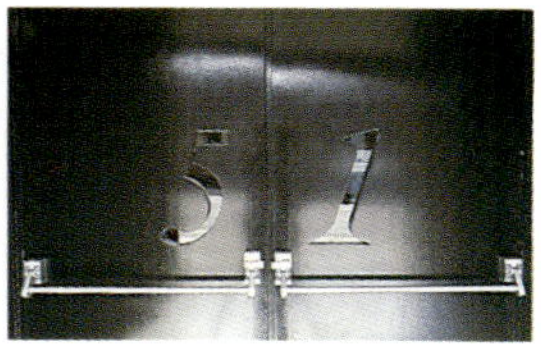
51
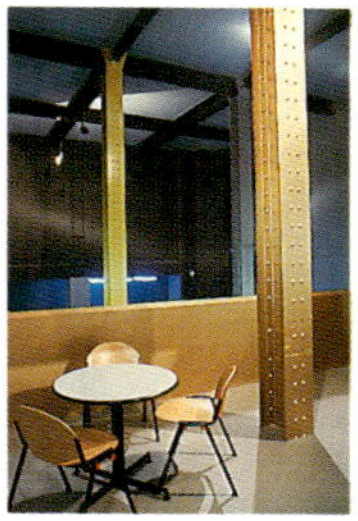
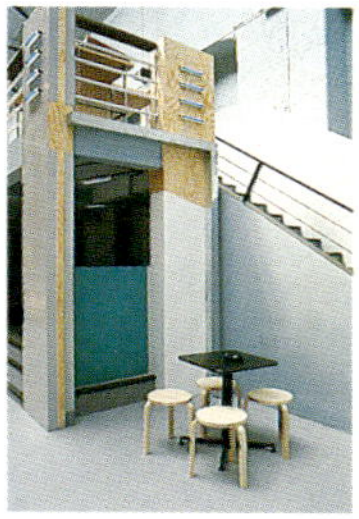
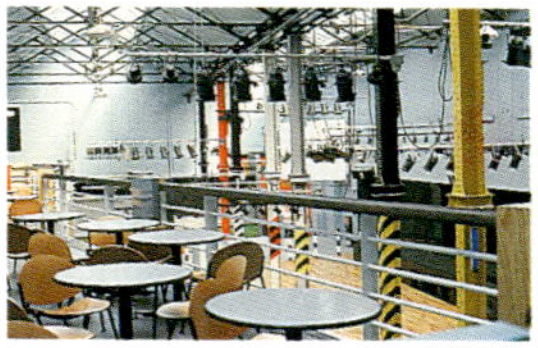
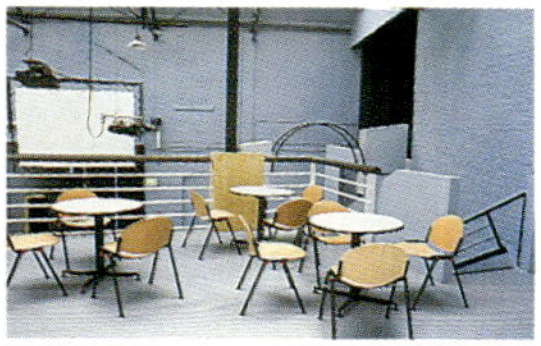
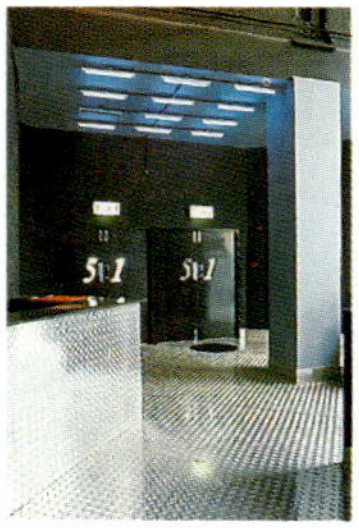
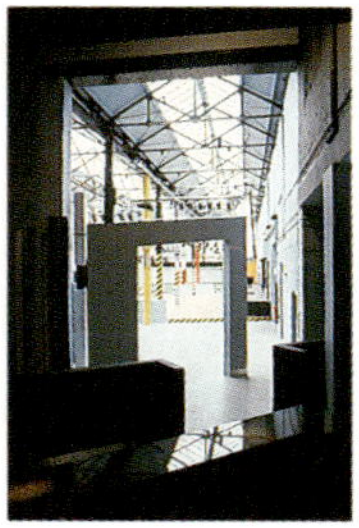
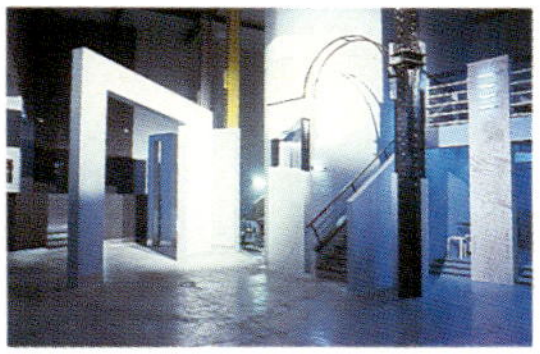
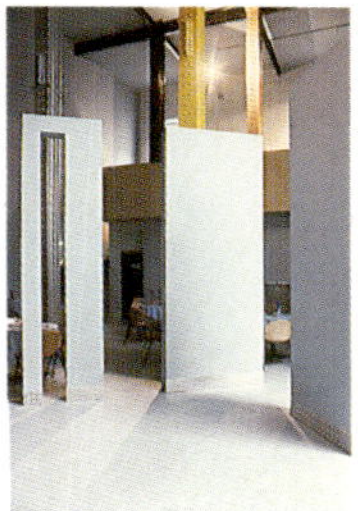
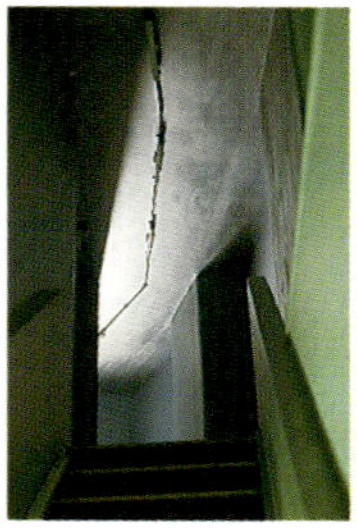
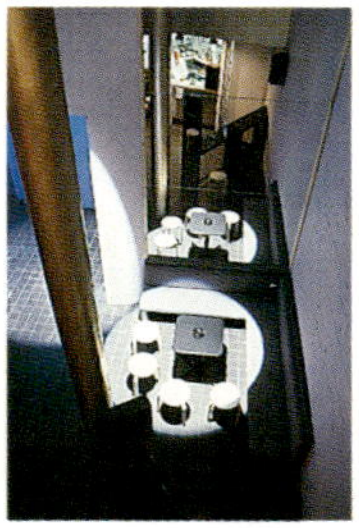
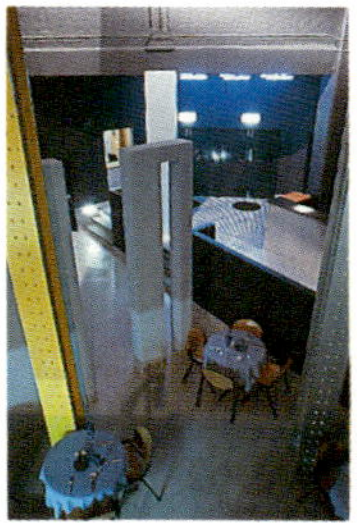
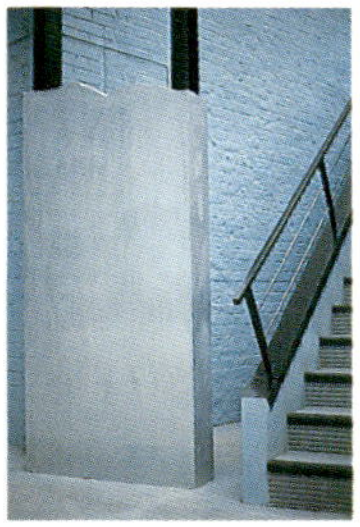

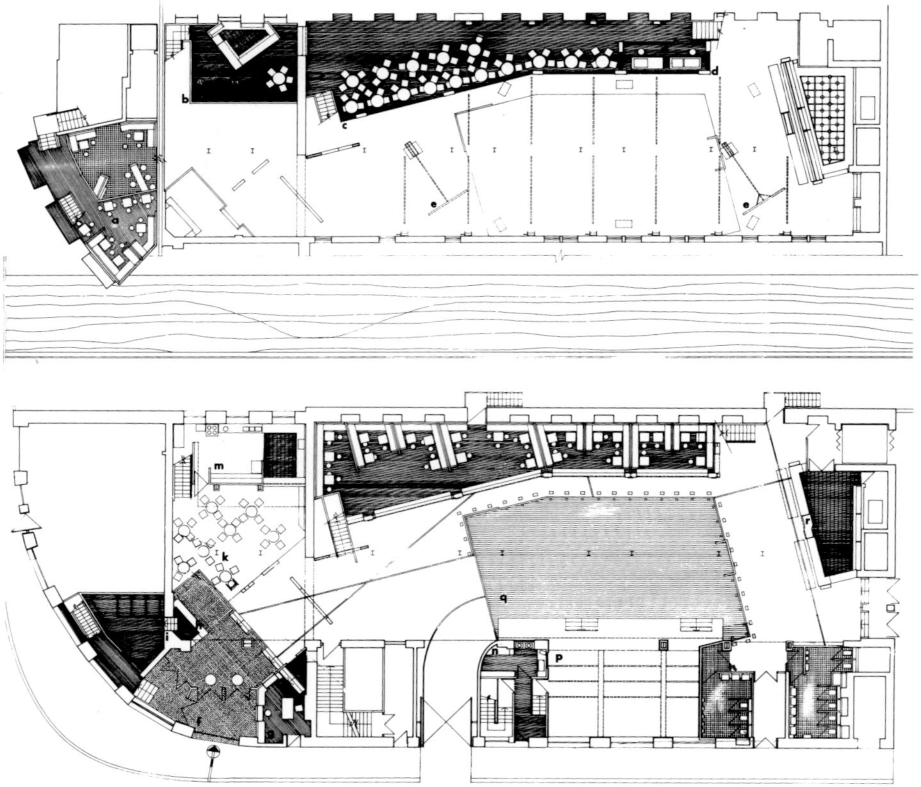

The Haçienda Fac51
Nightclub, Manchester, 1982.
The Haçienda is a 'community service', 'a space where things can happen', 'a place where people can meet'. Tony Wilson's views of four years ago may have changed slightly. It is now a serious business *and* a 'community service'. We originally wanted to 'create an environment which was visually stimulating, adaptable to a variety of activities, have flexibility within its framework to cope with changing ideas and attitudes, and initiate change within an environment which questions the language and values of the established disco/club format'. These were our preoccupations, perhaps only subconsciously, but they existed. Since 1982, The Haçienda has seen approximately one-and-a-quarter million people pass through the Fac51 doors. It has housed installations as varied and diverse as David Mach's magazine and vinyl record columns, Hannah Collins's life-size baroque staircase, the Zumbar swimming pool, Nude Night, and Peter Freeman's neon sculptures. It has staged performances from Madonna to Bernard Manning, William Burroughs to Vera Duckworth, The Smiths to Kraftwerk, Culture Club to New Order. Freefall tumblers, Psychic TV, trapeze artists, a circus and a fairground have all been embraced into the network of activities and entertainments provided by the diverse management, who have paid us our biggest and best compliment in saying that they have no need or desire to make any changes because they regard it as being timeless.
The 1990s beckon...

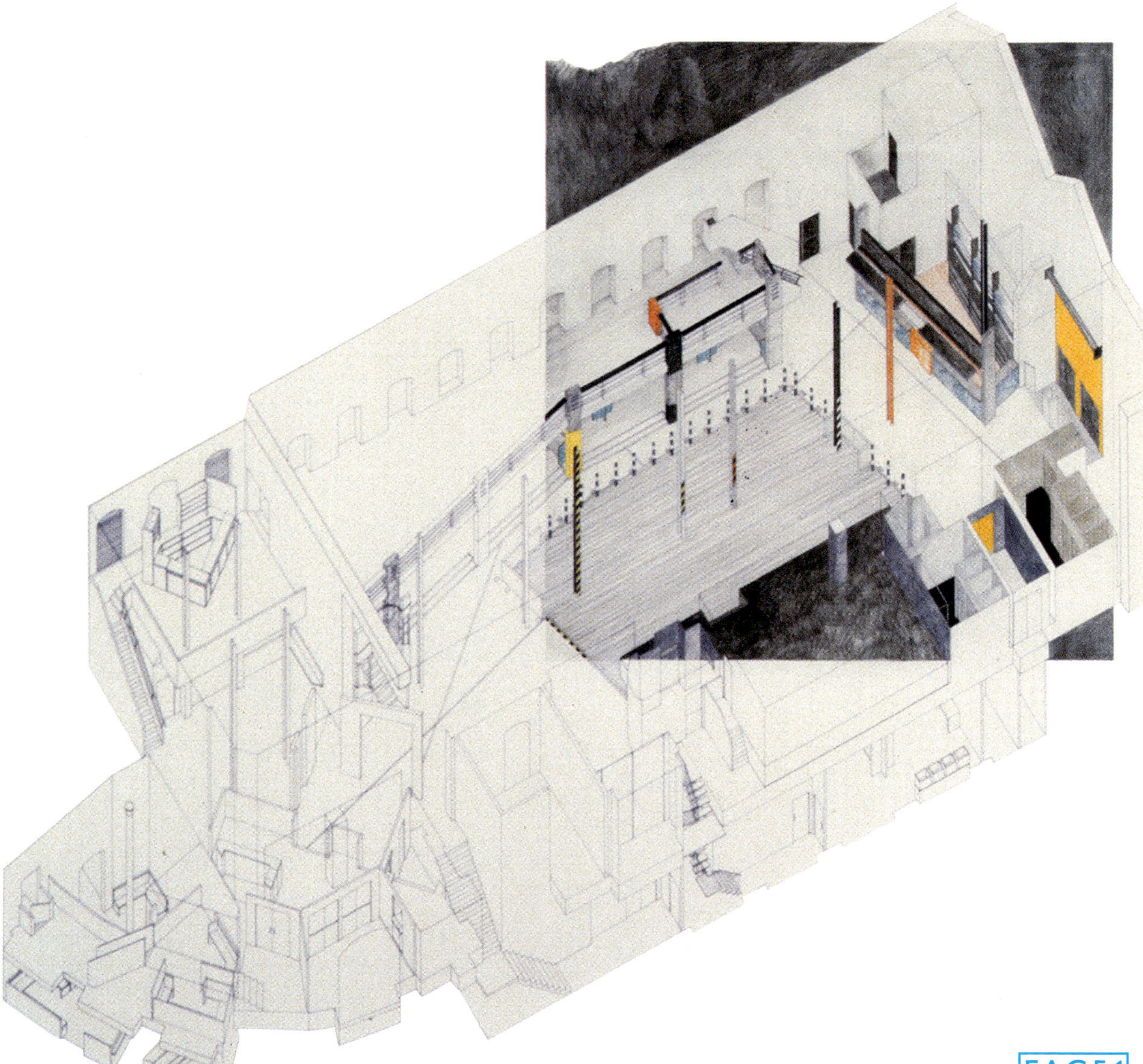

FAC 51
THE HAÇIENDA

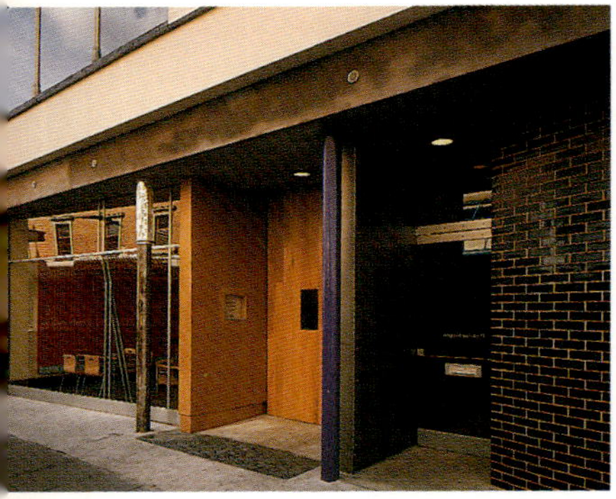

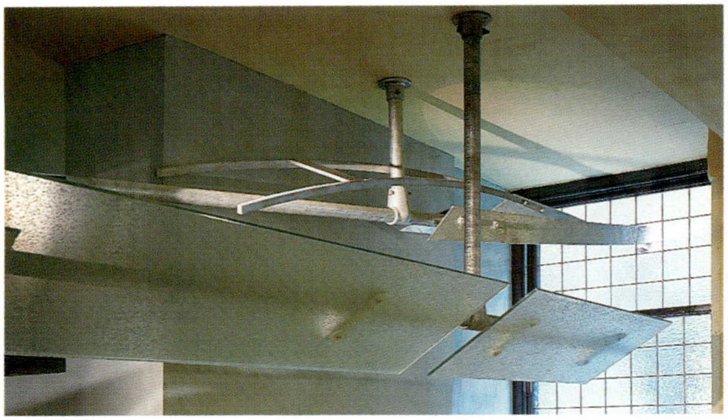

DRY Fac201
Bar conversion, Manchester, 1989. Dry is a permanent installation within the fabric of the existing shell. Nine hundred square metres of a former furniture warehouse on two floors, running from Oldham Street at the front to Spear Street at the rear have been converted into a 500 capacity bar, brasserie and all-purpose hangout. A 24-metre long slate and steel bar has been installed to serve from a menu including 15 vodkas and 57 malt whiskies. It is now possible to occupy space on Factory Communications territory during a 15-hour period, between The Haçienda and Dry.
Jasper Morrison furniture sits on a revived timber, concrete and terrazzo floor. Leaded windows have been renovated and retained, glazed bricks were kept and new ones introduced. As many original features as possible have been retained. We wanted to keep a sense of history, of Manchester's past; pre-Arndale Centre. The red plaster curtain was found behind hoardings, and has been restored and reinstated.
A found object, but not quite.

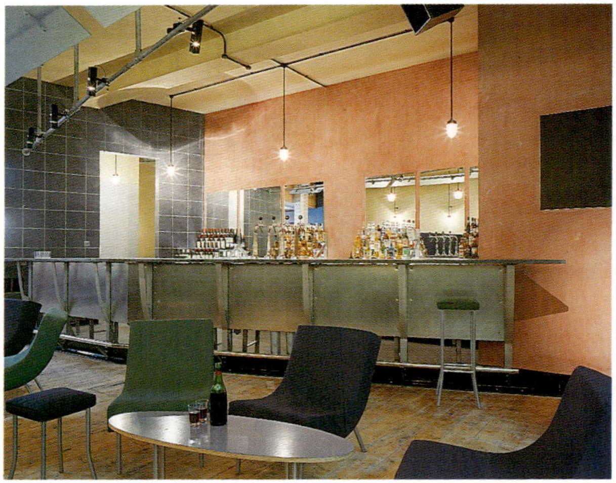

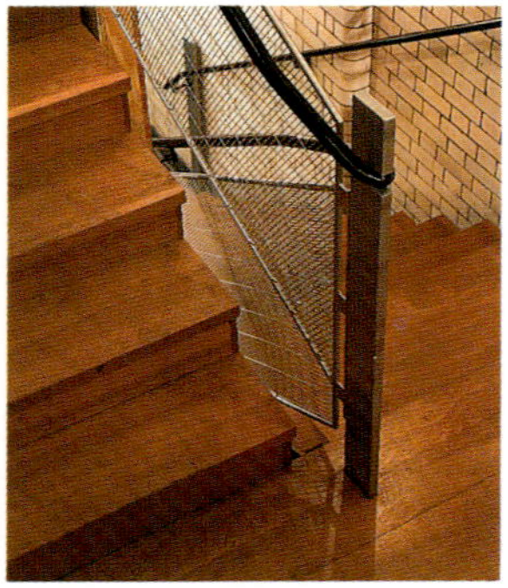

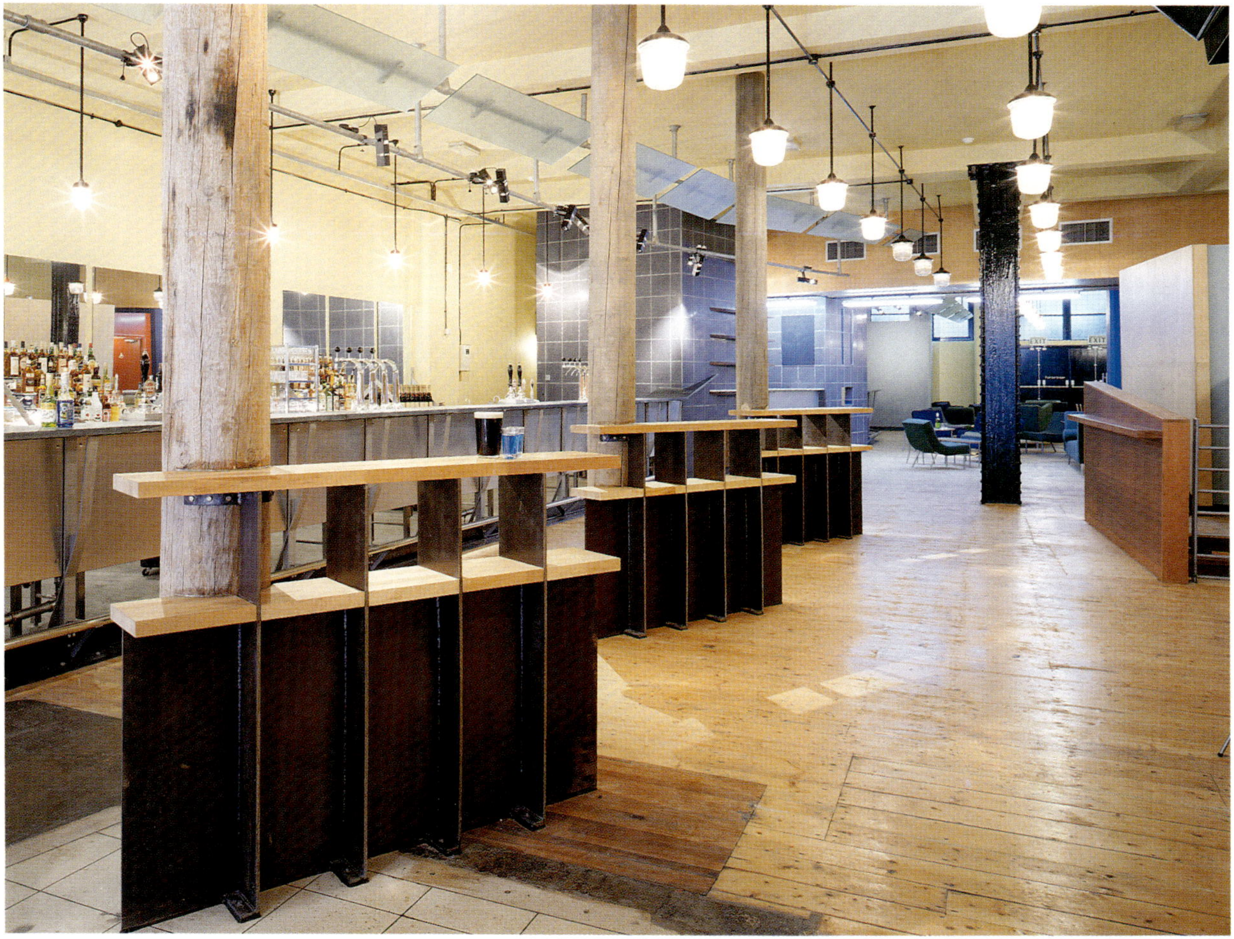

Specification:
Bead Blasted Stainless Steel, Delabole Blue Grey Slate, Acid Etched Coarse Stippled Glass, Douglas Fir, Japanese Fir, Japanese Oak, Utile, Junkers Beech, Black American Walnut, Telegraph Poles, Mirror Mosaic, Blue Glazed Bricks, Pantone 2685C Purple, International Orange, BS IOC33 Pollen, Galvanised Steel, Lapistone Marbo Tiles, Turquoise MG35 Glazed Tiles, PVF2 Silver, Polished Stainless Steel, Linen Finish Stainless Steel

Peter Mance

The Coming-and-Going Café

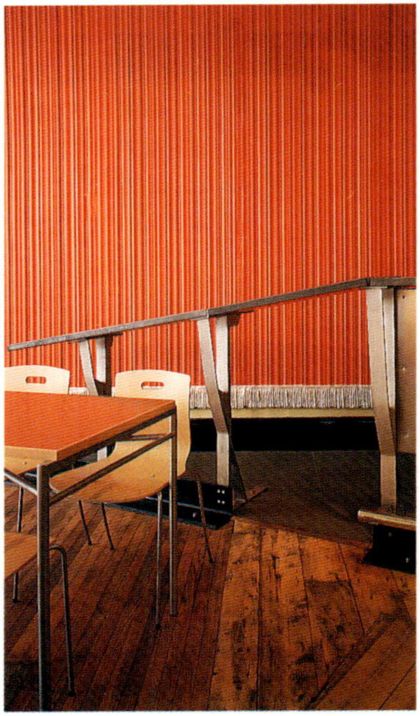

The Red Curtain...

DRY is a tall and long space. Nothing is hidden in this bar. DRY carries the daylight and street into itself. The bar is public, it has a shopfront. People are conspicuous to the street. The lighting level is sufficient to provide a clean sharp view of the interior's extent. The history of the building still exists. It has not been ignored. A large red fibrous plaster curtain has been frozen in time. A found piece, a relic from the former life of the building. It has been restored and re-exhibited.

Empty...

Restful, almost like a library. Any particular area can be occupied, you can sit, take coffee, beer, wine, read and not feel intimidated by being the only person in such a large bar. The environment allows different people to approach it without considering the nature of their surroundings. To feel that this place is for everyone, not an exclusive domain of fashion.

A few more people enter...

Slowly, the bar draws in more customers. Some in groups, some alone. DRY is a place to meet and talk. Like a continental bar or cafe, it is for conversations. It provides an opportunity for people to exchange ideas. The bar springs off the central kitchen enclosure to stretch from front to rear. It is lifted clear of the floor. Stainless steel uprights carry a 30mm thickness of Delabole slate. Drainage and support services are visible, their

Paul Mason

purpose and functions self-evident. This is a contemporary environment, where control and respect have brought about a place of encounters.

The bar is full...

Huge oak doors pivot. The evening brings the capacity crowd. The Coughtrie lights are dimmed, and the sound system given enough volume to provide competition to the exchange of Manchester's urban inhabitants. The immediate details recede. The ceiling landscape becomes apparent as a deliberate expression of services and lighting networks. Acid etched and stippled glass panels pivot on a steel rail above the full length of the slate bar. Two barbed steel spears pierce the front and rear glazing to become landmarks on Oldham Street and Spear Street. DRY***201***.

Another location...

DRY, the longest bar on the drawing board, coming to your town soon. Thank you, Manchester.

Dry was built to extend the Factory culture and to provide the Haçienda club clientele with somewhere to go in the early evening. When we researched the scheme we did not look to London for inspiration but to the cities of Barcelona and Los Angeles - to locations like Kate Mantalini's and the designs of Frank Gehry for Rebecca's Bar. The projected atmosphere was intended to encourage calm conversation. The bar also had to look and function well-packed or relatively quiet. The design team understood the importance of the translation of concepts by the client such as glass racking towers, underlit spirit shelves and a completely hidden glass washing area. All these things materialized into the project from fairly vague ideas and were executed exactly as the client imagined them. When DRY finally opened, the same clientele who enjoyed the Haçienda, immediately felt at ease in the building.

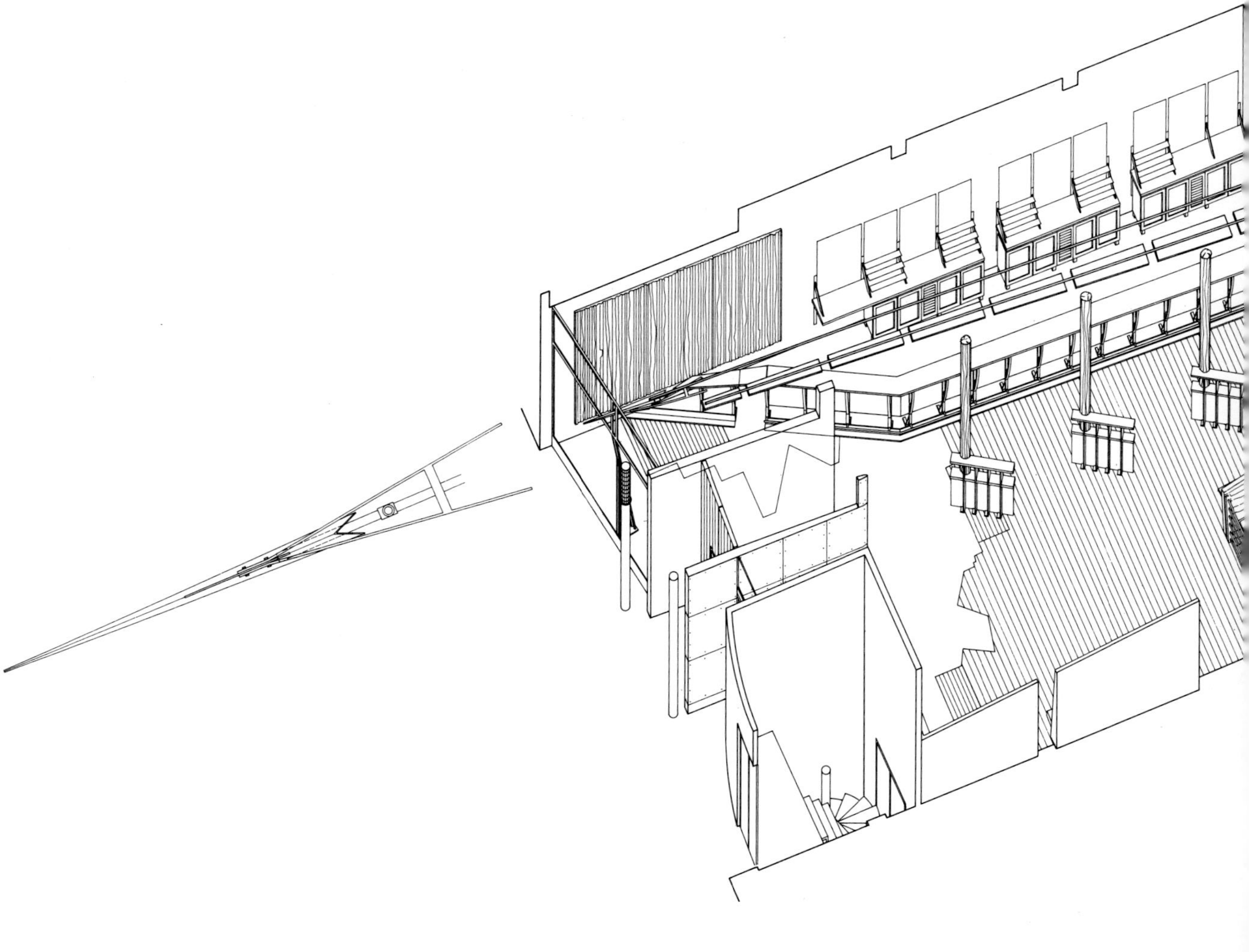

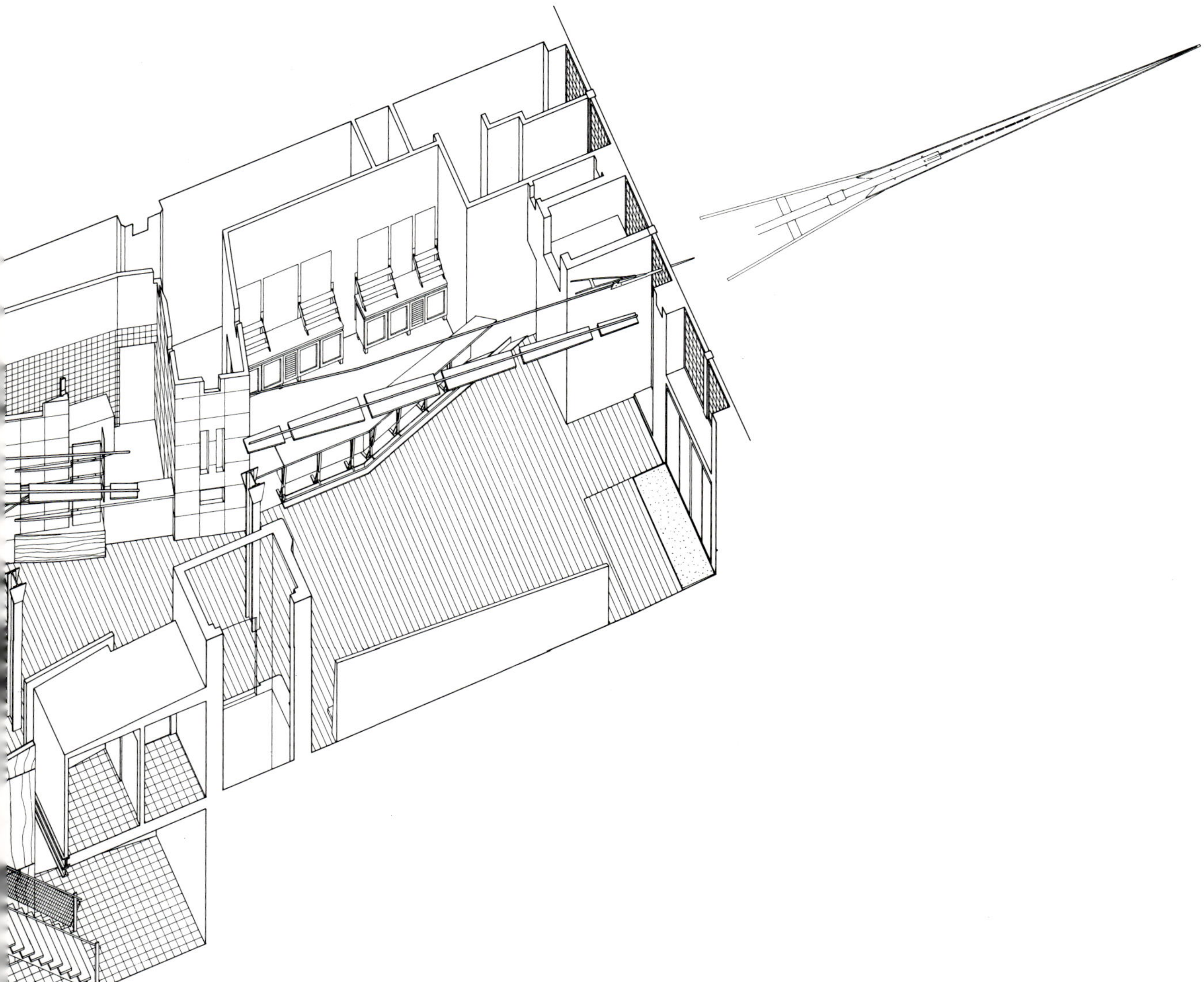

DRY**201**

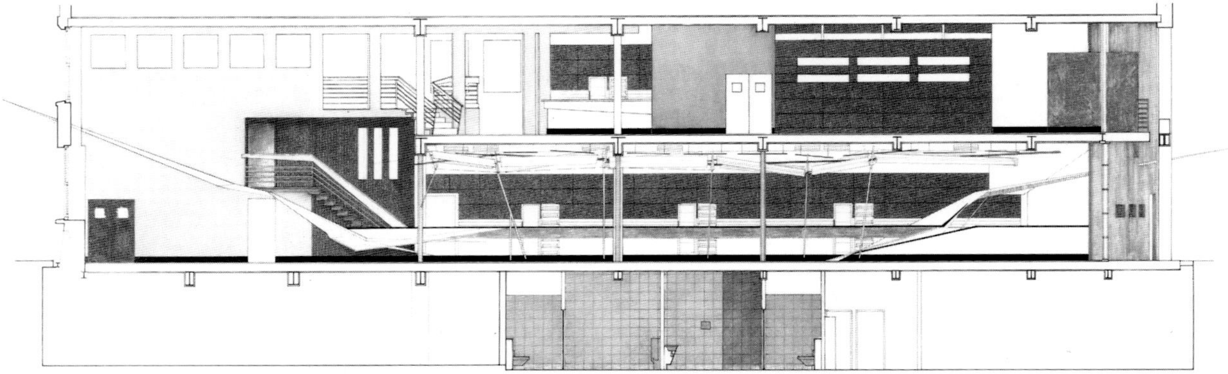

Proposed scheme for three floors

Completed scheme on two floors

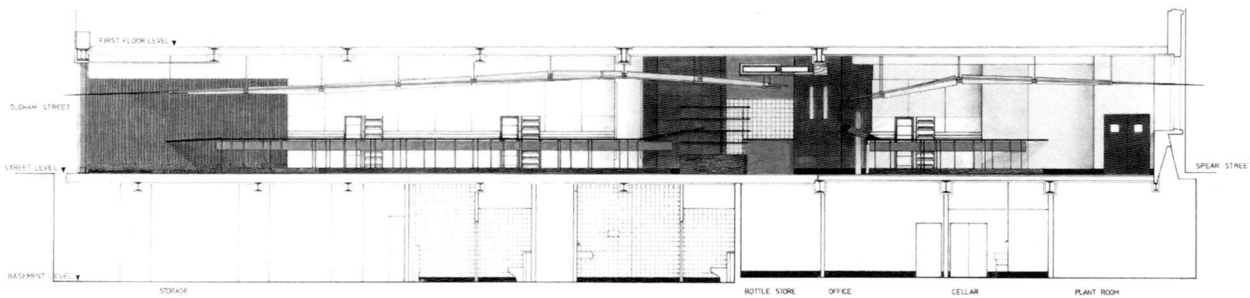

SECTION : AA

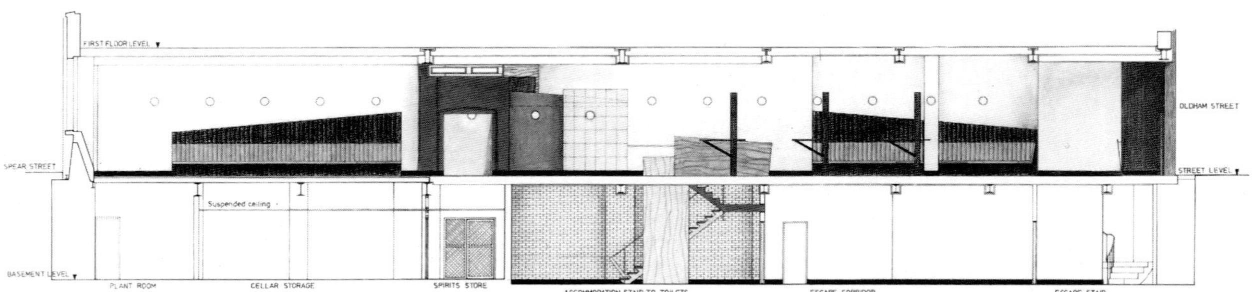

Elena Massucco

Dry is a bar on Oldham Street...

Word has reached us that on busy nights Dry afficionados will queue alongside the blue glazed brick wall on Oldham Street and wait to be admitted. The unthinkable has happened in Manchester - people are standing on line to drink. They are responding to something which has been commissioned, designed and executed especially for them. For designers this public expression is the highest compliment.

Prior to becoming a bar, the site was an empty yawning shell, windows boarded up, the smell of neglect lingering. I would stand at one end of the ground floor, look at the rear and try to imagine our ideas constructed. On the right, there would be the heart of the project - the bar itself. A monolithic kitchen interrupting the the run of slate and steel. Here the bar would flip up and stop, clamping itself to the Marbo tiled wall. Above the bar a travelling spear piercing the building from front to back like a piece of meat ready to be grilled. To the right, the seating areas with fitted banquettes and freestanding furniture. The existing lift shaft repossessed to accommodate the guts of the services which would spill out and snake round at ceiling level.

I could imagine the people circulating, entering the oversized oak entrance doors, sitting in the glazed frontage, propping up the bar, leaning against the telegraph poles, disappearing down the accommodation stairs to cluster at the bottom and gossip with the others coming out of the w.cs. I could imagine the living breathing space that it is now. Standing opposite the site on the other side of Oldham Street, the idea of a queue alongside the blue glazed bricks didn't enter my head.

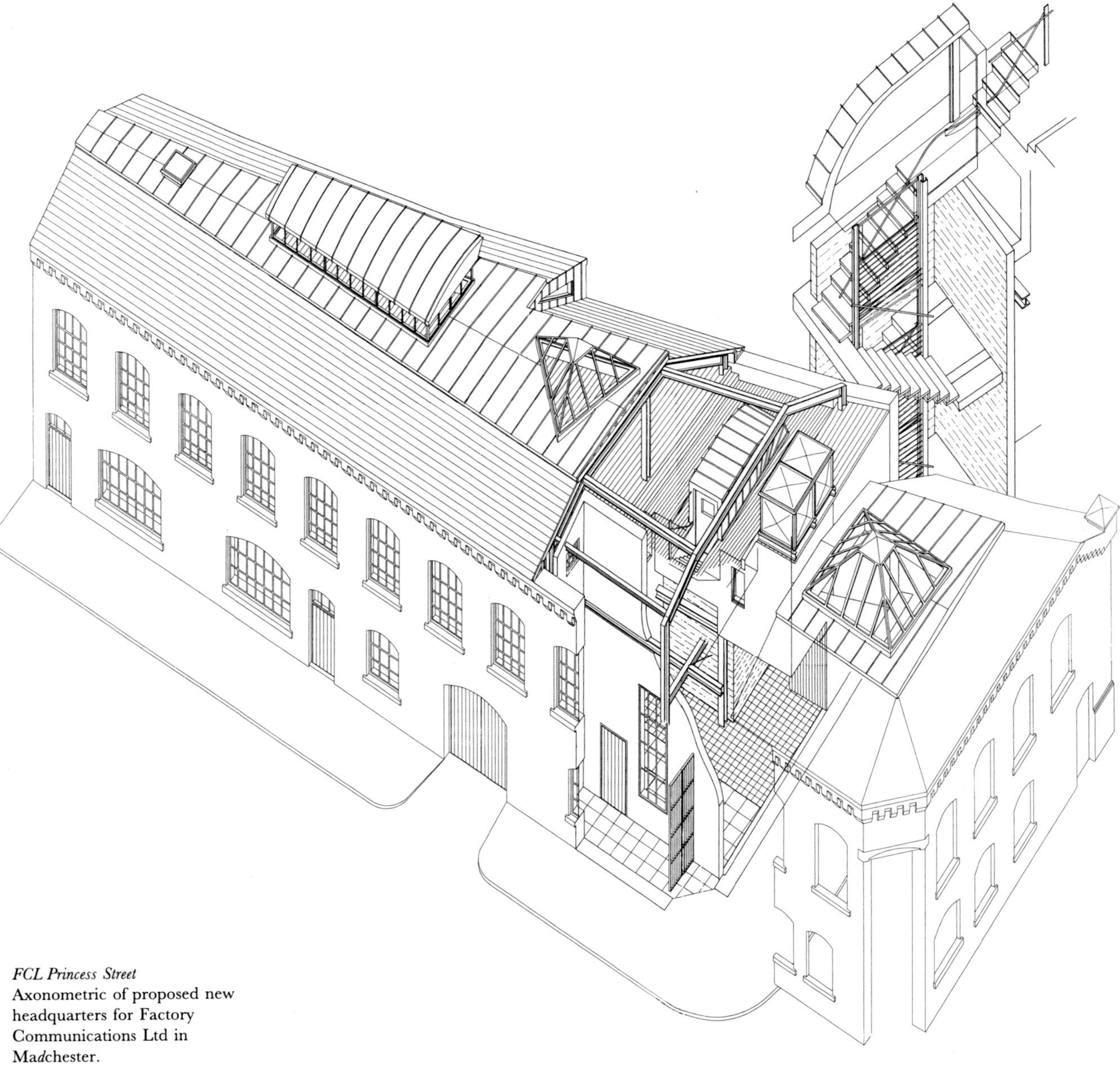

FCL Princess Street
Axonometric of proposed new headquarters for Factory Communications Ltd in Ma*d*chester.

Tony Wilson

Ben and Me

I hate his toilets. Don't get me wrong; I love HIS toilet. At home with Chrissie and Ben, if you want a piss, it's great, green slate and contours which outdo Manhattan's Royalton, having that Kelly subtlety so lately missing from the late Rubell's over-designed palace. No, its just that I hate his toilets, plural. The ones he does for us, FCL. Maybe it was the metallic silver paint which five minutes after the Haçienda opened in May 1983 was exuding sweat like a blousy *Hausfrau* on 'Hit Man and Her'. It could be me of course, everybody else seems to love the pale blue tiles of the DRY loos. Pale Blue? Yes, it's just me; I bloody hate pale blue tiles. And my campaign for Saville Steel commodes. I've always felt that my failure in this vital matter of sourcing had an unhealthy amount to do with the ongoing debate about Orchestral Manoeuvres' first album sleeve. I enjoy the debate as much as the next man, as B. Kelly and P. Saville recount the night they drove to the Lynne Franks shop: 'I saw the door first'...'No. I did'. But as it effectively means I get stuck with white earthen-ware bogs, it does my head in. And do you wanna talk cloakrooms?

And, yes, I'm hiding. Hiding this critical essay behind critical jibes; in the same way that day to day, working with Ben 'mon semblable, mon frère', I hide my adulation behind cloakroom/toilet verbal assaults; 'gonna hang your coat up then, Ben? Huh?'.

Why. 'Cause adulation sounds prissy and adulation is the only word. I don't care about his supreme marshalling of materials; I don't care about his colour palette that sends the rest of the bastards back to their Pantone book; I don't even care about the perspective and sense of journey he gives to any room he happens to get his teeth into. I just care deeply that he can design something that is completely of the minute, architecture and design that reeks of the 'now' that people didn't even imagine half an hour ago; and that design, that architecture, seven years later, is still completely alive, still happening, still breathtaking, as if it had never taken breath.

Such talent makes me adulate...I adulate Ben Kelly. But what the fuck are you going to do; 'Hey Ben, you're my hero.' Forget it. So much easier to say, 'The toilets are shit again, you just can't do bloody toilets...What's the problem...anal retentive or is that just your hairstyle etc etc...'. Yep, better than adulation. And stainless steel bogs will be better for the new HQ building, Ben,...Ben..., have I won that one yet?

Yrs. Fat Willy

PROJECTS

Ben Kelly Student Projects

*Artbar**
Client: Royal College of Art Students' Union, Royal College of Art, Kensington, London
Completed 1973
Geoff Hollington, Ben Kelly

Chair Art
Client: Department. of Environmental Design, Royal College of Art
Completed: 1972/73
Geoff Hollington, Ben Kelly

Lafrance
Client: Magnett Bartlett/RCA
Completed: 1973
Geoff Hollington, Ben Kelly

A Ware, B Ware, Y Ware
Client: RCA (and sold privately)
Completed: 1975
Robin Levien, Geoff Hollington, Ben Kelly

Ben Kelly Design Project List

Howie
Client: Lynne Franks, Paul Howie
Covent Garden, London
Completed: 1977
Ben Kelly

Shopfront: clothes shop
Client: Seditionaries – Malcolm McLaren, Vivienne Westwood
King's Road, London
Completed: 1977/8
David Connor, Ben Kelly

Office conversion
Client: Malcolm McLaren/Glitterbest Ltd (Sex Pistols' management company)
Shaftesbury Avenue, London
Completed: 1978
Ben Kelly

Studio conversion
Sex Pistols' Rehearsal Studios
Client: Malcolm McLaren/Sex Pistols
Denmark Street, London
Completed: 1978
Ben Kelly

Clothes shop
Client: The Last Resort – Margaret and Mickey French
Goulston Street, London
Completed: 1979
Ben Kelly

Private flat
Client: Steve Jones (Sex Pistols' guitarist)
West Hampstead, London
Completed: 1979
Ben Kelly

Fashion exhibition
The Individual Clothes Show
Client: Wendy Booth, Leslie Goring
Athenaeum Hotel, Piccadilly, London
1979 and 1980
Ben Kelly

Stage equipment
Client: Orchestral Manœuvres in the Dark
OMD First Tour 1980
Ben Kelly

Dereta showroom
Client: Paul Howie
Market Place, London
Completed: 1980
Ben Kelly

Teamwork
Client: Lynne Franks, Paul Howie, Strawberry Studio
St. Christopher's Place, London
Completed: 1980
Ben Kelly, Gerard Murtagh

Clothes shop
Chatters
Client: John Tsiattalou
St. Christopher's Place, London
Completed: 1980
Ben Kelly

Office conversion
Client: Lynne Franks P.R.
Covent Garden, London
Completed: 1981
Ben Kelly

Office conversion
Client: Marysia Woronyska P.R.
Marylebone High Street, London
Completed: 1981/82
Ben Kelly

The Haçienda Fac51
Client: Factory Communications Ltd/Gainwest Ltd
11–13 Whitworth Street West, Manchester
Completed: 1982
Sandra Douglas, Ben Kelly

Photographer's studio
Client: Tony McGee
Farringdon Road, London
Completed: 1982
Sandra Douglas, Ben Kelly

It's All True
Arena documentary 1983
Client: BBC2 and Julian Temple
Ben Kelly, Julian Temple

TV set design
'Loose Talk' – Channel 4, 1983
Client: RPM (Production Co.), Steve Taylor
Ben Kelly

Smile
Client: Keith Wainwright, Leslie Russell
King's Road, London
Completed: 1983
Sandra Douglas, Ben Kelly

Private house
Client: Sandy and Tony McGee
Camden Town, London
Completed: 1984
Sandra Douglas, Ben Kelly

Sarah Dallas Studio
Client: Sarah Dallas, Knitwear company
Colne, Lancashire
Completed: 1984
Sandra Douglas, Ben Kelly

Bedroom and bathroom conversion
Client: Lulu and John Frieda
Hampstead: London
Completed: 1985
Sandra Douglas, Ben Kelly

Bathroom conversion
Client: Sue and Kevin Godley
Chertsey, Surrey
Completed: 1985
Simon Catchpole, Sandra Douglas, Ben Kelly

Medialab
Client: Medialab Video Production Company
Chelsea Wharf, London
Completed: 1985
Simon Catchpole, Sandra Douglas, Ben Kelly

Office
Client: Lynne Franks P.R.
Marble Arch, London
Completed 1986
Simon Catchpole, Sandra Douglas, Ben Kelly

Ladies WCs
Client: Sir Robert McAlpine/ Schroeder Wag Merchant Bankers
Cheapside, London
Completed: 1986
Robert Hardy, Ben Kelly

Private house
Client: Sandy and Tony McGee
Regent's Park, London
Completed: 1987
Sandra Douglas, Ben Kelly

Shard Mirror
Client: The Alma Furniture Company Ltd
Completed: 1987
Ben Kelly

Pickwick Clothing
Client: Pickwick Clothing Ltd
Quincy
Dean Street, London
Completed: 1987
Sandra Douglas, Ben Kelly, Peter Mance, Jackie Smith
Office/warehouse conversion
Prairie Street, Battersea, London
Completed: 1988
Denis Byrne, Sandra Douglas, Ben Kelly, Peter Mance, Elena Massucco
Quincy
Floral Street, Covent Garden, London
Completed: 1988
Sandra Douglas, Ben Kelly, Peter Mance, Elena Massucco

Clothes shop
Jenkyn Jones
Client: No Yes Ltd
Broadwick Street, Soho, London
Completed: 1988
Sandra Douglas, Ben Kelly, Louise King, Peter Mance, Elena Massucco

Private house
Client: Lynne Franks & Paul Howie
Little Venice, London
Completed: 1989
Sandra Douglas, Ben Kelly, Peter Mance, Elena Massucco

Dry Fac201
Client: Fac201 Ltd/Gainwest Ltd
Oldham Street, Manchester
Completed: 1989
Denis Byrne, Sandra Douglas, Ben Kelly, Louise King, Peter Mance, Elena Massucco

FCL Princess Street
Client: Factory Communications Ltd
Princess Street, Manchester
Completion: 1990
Denis Byrne, Sandra Douglas, Ben Kelly, Louise King, Peter Mance, Elena Massucco, Nick Toft

Office/warehouse conversion
Client: 4AD Ltd
Wandsworth, London
Completion: 1990
Sandra Douglas, Ben Kelly, Louise King, Peter Mance, Elena Massucco, Nick Toft

**Illustrated projects are in italic type*

RECORD SLEEVES

Orchestral Manœuvres in the Dark
Album cover
Perforated sleeve
Design: Ben Kelly, Peter Saville
Din Disc

Section 25
Girls don't count
7-inch single sleeve
Design: Ben Kelly
Art Direction: Peter Saville
Factory Records – Fac18

A Certain Ratio
Sextet
Album cover
Design: Ben Kelly
Sleeve Painting: Denis Ryan
Factory Records – Fact55

A Certain Ratio
Waterline
12-inch single sleeve
Design: Ben Kelly
Factory Records – Fac52

Godley and Creme
Ism Ism
Album cover
Perforated sleeve
Design: Ben Kelly
Polydor

Graham Parker
Another Grey Area
Album cover
Design: Ben Kelly
Sleeve Painting: Denis Ryan
Photography: Michael Halsband
RCA

The Boomtown Rats
V Deep
Album cover
Design: Ben Kelly
Photography: Jon Prew
Model Maker: Gary Wright
Letter Carving: Peter Foster
Phonogram

Graham Parker
Temporary Beauty
7-inch single sleeve
Design: Ben Kelly
RCA

The Cure
...happily ever after
Album cover
Design: Ben Kelly
A&M Records

The Boomtown Rats
Never in a Million Years
7-inch single sleeve
Design: Ben Kelly
Phonogram

The Boomtown Rats
House on Fire
7-inch and 12-inch single sleeves
Design: Ben Kelly, Brett Wickens
Phonogram

The Boomtown Rats
Charmed Lives
7-inch and 12-inch single sleeves
Design: Ben Kelly, Brett Wickens
Phonogram

The Cure
Pornography
Album cover
Design: Ben Kelly
Photography: Michael Kostiff
A&M Records

UB40
UB40 1980-83
Album cover
Design: Ben Kelly
Photography: Jon Prew
A&M Records

RPM
In Colour (USA Release)
Album cover
Design: Ben Kelly
Photography: Jon Prew
A&M Records

BIBLIOGRAPHY

Publications

Actuel, Orchestral Manœuvres in the Dark album cover featured, 5 March 1980

Alastair Best, 'Baring the Bones', *Designers' Journal*, March 1989

Alastair Best, 'Night Club, Manchester', *The Architectural Review*, September 1982

Blueprint, 'Quincey & Jones' [sic] November 1988

Kate Braithwaite, 'Steel Yourself', *Daily Express*, 16 September 1989

Allan Campbell, 'Intro 4', *The Face*, September 1989

Design, 'Record Sleeve Revival', July 1980

Designers' Journal, 'Preview 89', January 1989

Design Week, 'Ben Kelly wipes up Dry Bar', July 1989

Design Week, 'Invasion of the Oldham Street Winos', September 1989

Disco Mirror & Licensed Design, 'Dry-arid attitudes from Ben Kelly Design', September 1989

Jonathan Glancey, 'Drawn into Interiors', *The Architectural Review*, March 1984

Judi Goodwin, 'Manchester's Gothic Façades hide an intimate and stylish city', *Elle Decoration*, Autumn 1989

Robert Graham/Andy Spinoza, 'Doing the Haçienda Hustle', *City Life Manchester*, 17–31 May 1985

Dinah Hall, 'High Tech at Home', *Cosmopolitan*, May 1979

Dylan Jones, 'The Art of Shopping', *Arena*, Winter 1988/89

James Kirklington, 'Hairstyle, *The World of Interiors*, November 1984

Jane Lamacraft, 'Kelly & Toms', *Designers' Journal*, January 1988

Manchester Evening News, 'Tied to the Factory', 5 January 1989

Jose Manser, 'High & Dry', *Designers' Journal*, October 1989

Penny McGuire, 'Journey into the Interior', *Designer*, February 1984

Guy Nelson, 'Now Open: Bar', *The Independent*, 24 July 1989

Katie Neville, 'Night Moves, Right Moves', *Harpers & Queen*, August 1983

Rick Poyner, 'Dry Run', *Blueprint*, September 1989

Liz Smith, 'A Snip in the King's Road', *The Standard*, 1 November 1983

Andy Spinoza, 'Biggest Bar in Town', *Manchester Evening News*, 29 July 1989

The Sunday Express Magazine, 'Cover Story', 17 February 1985

Steve Taylor, 'New Steps for the Leisure Industry', *The Face*, August 1982

Jane Withers, 'Activists', *The World of Interiors*, March 1989

The World of Interiors, 'Activists', April 1988

Books

Iwona Blazwick, *An Endless Adventure...An Endless Passion... An Endless Banquet: A Situationists' Scrapbook* ICA V Verso, 1989

Edward Booth-Clibborn, *The Best of British Corporate Design*, Internos Books, 1989

British Design & Art Direction 1981, *The 19th Annual of the Best British Graphics, Advertising, Television, and Editorial Design*, The Designers & Art Directors Association of London, 1981

Roger Dean and David Howells, *The 2nd Vol. Album Cover Album*, Paper Tiger, 1982

Catherine McDermott, *Street Style: British Design in the 80s*, Design Council, 1987

EXHIBITIONS

British Illustration from Caxton to Chloe
British Council touring exhibition, Royal College of Art, October 1986, Exhibit 313 – drawing of Smile, hairdressing salon, King's Road, Chelsea, London. Video accompanied exhibition showing execution of drawing for Smile.

British Design – New Traditions
Portal No. 1, Boymans Van-Beuningen Museum, Rotterdam. March – May 1989

British Design in Vienna
Kunstlerhaus Galleries, Vienna, Central Office of Information sponsored Exhibition, British Council, April 1986

Inside
Exhibition of drawings of interiors, Glasgow School of Art, January 1987

The Situationists
ICA Galleries, London, 1989

Jury
1985, 1990 D & AD Design for Retail & Environmental jury

AWARDS

D & AD (Designers & Art Directors) Association,
1981 Silver Awards
Most outstanding album sleeve range
Most outstanding sleeve poster
Orchestral Manœuvres in the Dark, Ben Kelly/Peter Saville
Most outstanding record sleeve sponsored by the record business
Section 25, *Girls don't count,*
Ben Kelly/Peter Saville

Music & Video Week Award
Sleeve Design 1980 (Popular full-price album)
Orchestral Manœuvres in the Dark, Ben Kelly/Peter Saville

Designers Journal
1990 First Equal Award, catagory B (schemes with contract price between £100,000 and £500,000)

CREDITS

Photographs
David Bache, David Bradfield, Geoff Beeckman, *Blueprint,* Richard Bryant, Peter Cook, Lyn Dale, Clive Frost, Denis Gilbert, Andrew Griffiths, Island Visual Arts, Trevor Key, Ben Kelly, Tony McGee, Luciana Martinez, Carol Moss, Sydney W. Newbery, Julie Phipps, Jon Prew, Tony Stokes, David Watts, Alan Williams, Larry Williams, and Sprengel Museum (Hannover) for Schwitters' *Merzbau*

Text
The quotation on page 65 is from Christopher Gray, ed., trans., *Leaving the Twentieth Century: the Incomplete Work of the Situationists International,* Freefall Publications, 1974. © Christopher Gray, who we have been unable to contact.

ACKNOWLEDGEMENTS

To the 'guest list' for their time and words; Factory Communications for the colour of their money; Peter Saville Associates for the look of the book; Jon Prew for his photos; Island Visual Arts; Anthony d'Offay Gallery, Richard Long and Bruce McLean for supplying original material otherwise impossible to obtain; Francis Kyle Gallery for attempting to trace Andrew Griffiths.
To Catherine McDermott for instigating the project, cajoling the guest list and for her support and creative steering through the pages of this book.

This book is dedicated to Doreen, Herbert, Chrissie and Liam

AN ADT DESIGNFILE

Architecture Design and
Technology Press
128 Long Acre
London WC2E 9AN
A Division of
Longman Group UK Limited

First published 1990

British Library Cataloguing in Publication Data: A CIP catalogue record for this book is available from the British Library

ISBN 1 85454 052 1

Art direction:
Peter Saville Associates
Design:
Jonathan Moberly

Typeset in 8 point Adobe Neue Helvetica 45 and 7.5 point Monotype Baskerville, leaded to 9 points. Designed and paged entirely on an Apple Macintosh II using Quark Xpress, McView and OmniPage. The form of this book was only made possible using this technology.

Linotronic:
Patrick at Alphabet Set

Reproduced, printed and bound in Hong Kong on 140gsm Topkote Gloss Art